A ROUNDUP

OF COWBOY HUMOR

W7-CGH-561

A ROUNDUP
OF COWBOY HUMOR

Edited by Ted Stone

Roundup
BOOKS

Red Deer College Press

The Publishers
Red Deer College Press
56 Avenue & 32 Street Box 5005
Red Deer Alberta Canada T4N 5H5

Acknowledgments
Cover art and design by Kurt Hafso
Text design by Dennis Johnson
Printed and bound in Canada by Parkland ColorPress
for Red Deer College Press
Special thanks to Vicki Mix for her assistance in the preparation of this book
5 4 3 2 1

Financial support provided by the Alberta Foundation for the Arts, a beneficiary
of the Lottery Fund of the Government of Alberta, and by the Canada Council,
the Department of Canadian Heritage and Red Deer College.

COMMITTED TO THE DEVELOPMENT OF CULTURE AND THE ARTS

Canadian Cataloguing in Publication Data

A roundup of cowboy humor
(Roundup books)
ISBN 0-88995-141-1
1. Western stories. 2. Humorous stories, American. 3. American
fiction—20th century. 4. Cowboys—Fiction. I. Stone, Ted, 1947–
II. Series: Roundup books (Red Deer, Alta.)
PS648.W4R68 1995 813'.08740805 C95-910459-3

NOTE
To preserve the variety of writing styles reproduced in this collection, all
original spellings, punctuation and grammar have been retained.

Acknowledgments

"The Moon Dance Skunk" from *The Big It and Other Stories* by A.B. Guthrie. Copyright © 1960 by A.B. Guthrie, Jr. Reprinted by permission of Houghton Mifflin Co.

The story "Ol Antoine's Wooden Overcoat" from *Smith and Other Events* by Paul St. Pierre, © 1985, published by Douglas & McIntyre. Reprinted by permission.

"Champs at the Chuckabug," "Purt Near!" and "Rain on the Range" by S. Omar Barker are used by permission of Robert Phillips.

"A Savage Santa Claus," from *Trails Plowed Under* by Charles M. Russell, copyright © 1927 by Doubleday, a division of Bantam Doubleday Dell Publishing Group, Inc. Used by permission of Doubleday, a division of Bantam Doubleday Dell Publishing Group, Inc.

"It Was Just a Habit," Chapter One, *The Autobiography of Will Rogers,* edited by Donald Day. Copyright 1949 by Rogers Company. Copyright © renewed 1977 by Donald Day and Beth Day.

"Diary of a Steer," from *Cowboys Are Partly Human* by John R. Erickson © 1983. Used by permission of Gulf Publishing Company.

"The Disgraceful Affair of Turpentine Jackson," from *Tales of the Southwest* by Benjamin Capps. Copyright © 1991 by Benjamin Capps. Used by permission of Doubleday, a division of Bantam Doubleday Dell Publishing Group, Inc.

"The Legend of Boastful Bill," Charles Badger Clark, Jr. Reprinted, by permission, from *Sun and Saddle Leather,* Richard G. Badger, Publisher.

"Pecos Bill Invents Modern Cowpunching" from *Pecos Bill: The Greatest Cowboy of All Time* by James Cloyd Bowman. Copyright © 1937, 1964 by Albert Whitman & Company. All rights reserved. Used by permission.

"Ranch Truck" from the book *Laugh Kills Lonesome and Other Poems* by Mike Logan. Used by permission.

"The Punchers Tell a Few" from *Cowboy* by Ross Santee © 1977, Bison Books, University of Nebraska Press.

For Will Rogers
–T.S.

Contents

Introduction / 9

A Corner in Horses *by* STEWART EDWARD WHITE / 12

Pimienta Pancakes *by* O. HENRY / 24

When Bob Got Throwed *by* ANONYMOUS / 35

The Moon Dance Skunk *by* A.B. GUTHRIE / 37

Ol Antoine's Wooden Overcoat *by* PAUL ST. PIERRE / 46

Champs at the Chuckabug *by* S. OMAR BARKER / 70

Rain on the Range *by* S. OMAR BARKER / 84

Science at Heart's Desire *by* EMERSON HOUGH / 86

Ranch Truck *by* MIKE LOGAN / 99

A Savage Santa Claus *by* CHARLES M. RUSSELL / 102

It Was Just a Habit *by* WILL ROGERS / 107

How Jack Rainey Quit *by* ALFRED HENRY LEWIS / 122

When the Cook Fell Ill *by* B.M. BOWER / 131

The Punchers Tell a Few *by* ROSS SANTEE / 149

"Purt Near!" *by* S. OMAR BARKER / 157

Diary of a Steer *by* JOHN R. ERICKSON / 159

The Disgraceful Affair of Turpentine Jackson *by* BENJAMIN CAPPS / 164

The Legend of Boastful Bill *by* CHARLES BADGER CLARK, JR. / 171

Pecos Bill Invents Modern Cowpunching *by* JAMES CLOYD BOWMAN / 174

The Cloud Puncher *by* WILLIAM CUNNINGHAM / 186

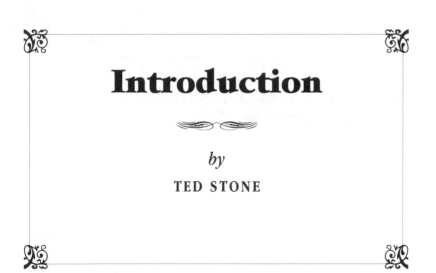

Introduction

by

TED STONE

N O COLLECTION OF HUMOROUS WRITING should begin with a long, serious introduction. Few people interested in reading books of humor, cowboy or any other kind, care much about the editorial considerations necessary to create them. They just want to read stories that will make them laugh, and a story's or poem's power to make me laugh was the main criterion for choosing what went into this book.

I did not limit the collection to any particular form of humor, so long as it was of the cattle country. Likewise, I made no special attempt to include particular time periods or styles of writing. And I certainly never tried to organize the stories to fit some profound theory of comic writing. On that score, I go along with Mark Twain when he said that analyzing comedy is like dissecting a frog: You can cut it up into pieces to see what makes it work, but the thing dies in the process.

For the most part, I avoided excerpts from novels when choosing these stories even though a lot of funny cowboy stories can be found in novels. For this collection, I wanted stories designed to stand on their own, stories in which the reader wouldn't need to know anything from earlier in a book to appreciate the comedy of a tale.

Apparent exceptions can be explained. Ross Santee's "The Punchers Tell a Few" is from the novel *Cowboy,* but the book is really a collection of short stories that happen to tell a longer tale. The same can be said about James Cloyd Bowman's "Pecos Bill Invents Modern Cowpunching." "It Was Just a Habit," the first chapter from Will Rogers' autobiography, is also included in this collection, even though it does not fall within the conventional definition of a short story. But no collection of cowboy humor would be complete without something from this great American humorist. Likewise, no collection of cowboy humor would be complete without a sampling of cowboy poetry. So poems, too, can be found in these pages.

Cowboy stories and poems come in all styles, but even when they're written down they tend to resemble oral tales. They're often the kind of stories once told beside campfires on roundups and trail drives, and the kind still told today in the ranching country of North America. Because humor is regularly a part of these oral stories, it's only natural that written cowboy stories, too, often raise a chuckle.

It's also to be expected that more than a few cowboys would graduate from campfire yarns to comic writing. Will Rogers and Charlie Russell are perhaps the most well-known cowboys turned writers represented in this collection. But Western literature has plenty of others. Indeed, most of the authors in this book come from Western farm or ranch backgrounds. Their stories span the more than one hundred years of cattle ranching in the North American West.

Even before the turn of the century, Alfred Henry Lewis wrote and published his classic book of comic yarns *Wolfville Days.* Lewis, whose story "How Jack Rainey Quit" appears in this collection, was perhaps the first writer to make fun of the violence common in the early days of the West. In succeeding years, humor became such a common element in cowboy stories that even the formula shoot-

'em-ups often included a comic sidekick to accompany the cowboy hero. Sometimes the heroes themselves even display humorous qualities. Prominent early twentieth century writers in this collection, such as B.M. Bower, Stewart Edward White and Emerson Hough, often took lighthearted rides with their cowboy heroes. O. Henry, known most for his stories of city life, began his writing career while serving time in a Texas jail, and he wrote several comic stories with cowboy characters. Indeed, his characteristic twists of plot seem particularly suited for the humorous Western tale.

Humor also figured prominently in the stories of S. Omar Barker, who wrote during the heyday of magazine pulp fiction. It was a time, perhaps, when the tradition of comic Western fiction was at low ebb, but Barker's tales consistently reflected the humanity and humor of Western life instead of the six-gun dramas more popular at that time.

As the pulp magazines declined at midcentury, comic cowboy tales regained some of the prominence they once held in novels and short stories. Examples in this collection include "The Moon Dance Skunk" by A.B. Guthrie, "Ol Antoine's Wooden Overcoat" by Paul St. Pierre and "The Disgraceful Affair of Turpentine Jackson" by Benjamin Capps. Although all of these stories were published in the latter half of the twentieth century, each of them falls clearly in the tradition of the comic Western yarn.

In the West, perhaps more than other areas of North America, the comic yarn has been more than just a form of storytelling or another aspect of entertainment. It's an integral part of everyday life, ingrained in the Western character like wrinkles on an old rancher's face. Humorous tales of the cattle country have been told and retold, written down and read, in poetry and prose, since cowboys first followed cattle north out of Texas in the 1860s. They will undoubtedly continue to be told as long as cattle and ranchers remain in the West. The stories in this collection are part of that tradition.

A Corner
in Horses

by
STEWART EDWARD WHITE

I T WAS DARK NIGHT. The stray-herd bellowed frantically from one of the big corrals; the cow-and-calf-herd from a second. Already the remuda, driven in from the open plains, scattered about the thousand acres of pasture. Away from the conveniences of fence and corral, men would have had to patrol all night. Now, however, everyone was gathered about the camp fire.

Probably forty cowboys were in the group, representing all types, from old John, who had been in the business forty years, and had punched from the Rio Grande to the Pacific, to the Kid, who would have given his chance of salvation if he could have been taken for ten years older than he was. At the moment Jed Parker was holding forth to his friend Johnny Stone in reference to another old crony who had that evening joined the roundup.

"Johnny," inquired Jed with elaborate gravity, and entirely ignoring the presence of the subject of conversation, "what is that thing just beyond the fire, and where did it come from?"

Johnny Stone squinted to make sure.

"That?" he replied. "Oh, this evenin' the dogs see something run down a hole, and they dug it out, and that's what they got."

The newcomer grinned.

"The trouble with you fellows," he proffered, "is that you're so plumb alkalied you don't know the real thing when you see it."

"That's right," supplemented Windy Bill drily. *"He* come from New York."

"No!" cried Jed. "You don't say so? Did he come in one box or in two?"

Under cover of the laugh, the newcomer made a raid on the dutch ovens and pails. Having filled his plate, he squatted on his heels and fell to his belated meal. He was a tall, slab-sided individual, with a lean, leathery face, a sweeping white moustache, and a grave and sardonic eye. His leather chaps were plain and worn, and his hat had been fashioned by time and wear into much individuality. I was not surprised to hear him nick-named Sacatone Bill.

"Just ask him how he got that game foot," suggested Johnny Stone to me in an undertone. So, of course, I did not.

Later someone told me that the lameness resulted from his refusal of an urgent invitation to return across a river. Mr. Sacatone Bill happened not to be riding his own horse at the time.

The Cattleman dropped down beside me a moment later.

"I wish," said he in a low voice, "we could get that fellow talking. He is a queer one. Pretty well educated apparently. Claims to be writing a book of memoirs. Sometimes he will open up in good shape, and sometimes he will not. It does no good to ask him direct, and he is as shy as an old crow when you try to lead him up to a subject. We must just lie low and trust to Providence."

A man was playing on the mouth organ. He played excellently well, with all sorts of variations and frills. We smoked in silence. The deep rumble of the cattle filled the air with its diapason. Always the shrill coyotes raved out in the mesquite. Sacatone Bill had finished his meal, and had gone to sit by Jed Parker, his old friend. They talked together low-voiced. The evening grew, and the eastern sky silvered over the mountains in anticipation of the moon.

Sacatone Bill suddenly threw back his head and laughed. "Reminds me of the time I went to Colorado!" he cried.

"He's off!" whispered the Cattleman.

A dead silence fell on the circle. Everybody shifted position the better to listen to the story of Sacatone Bill.

About ten year ago I got plumb sick of punchin' cows around my part of the country. She hadn't rained since Noah, and I'd forgot what water outside a pail or a trough looked like. So I scouted around inside of me to see what part of the world I'd jump to, and as I seemed to know as little of Colorado and minin' as anything else, I made up the pint of bean soup I call my brains to go there. So I catches me a buyer at Benson and turns over my pore little bunch of cattle and prepared to fly. The last day I hauled up about twenty good buckets of water and threw her up against the cabin. My buyer was setting his hoss waitin' for me to get ready. He didn't say nothin' until we'd got down about ten mile or so.

"Mr. Hicks," says he, hesitatin' like, "I find it a good rule in this country to overlook other folks' plays, but I'd take it mighty kind if you'd explain those actions of yours with the pails of water."

"Mr. Jones," says I, "it's very simple. I built that shack five year ago, and it's never rained since. I just wanted to settle in my mind whether or not that damn roof leaked."

So I quit Arizona, and in about a week I see my reflection in the winders of a little place called Cyanide in the Colorado mountains.

Fellows, she was a bird. They wasn't a pony in sight, nor a squar' foot of land that wasn't either street or straight up. It made me plumb lonesome for a country where you could see a long ways even if you didn't see much. And this early in the evenin' they wasn't hardly anybody in the streets at all.

I took a look at them dark, gloomy, old mountains, and a sniff at a breeze that would have frozen the whiskers of hope, and I made a dive for the nearest lit winder. They was a sign over it that just said:

THIS IS A SALOON

I was glad they labelled her. I'd never have known it. They had a fifteen-year-old kid tendin' bar, no games goin', and not a soul in the place.

"Sorry to disturb your repose, bub," says I, "but see if you can sort out any rye among them collections of sassapariller of yours."

I took a drink, and then another to keep it company—I was beginnin' to sympathise with anythin' lonesome. Then I kind of sauntered out to the back room where the hurdy-gurdy ought to be. Sure enough, there was a girl settin' on the pianner stool, another in a chair, and a nice shiny Jew drummer danglin' his feet from a table. They looked up when they see me come in, and went right on talkin'.

"Hello, girls!" says I.

At that they stopped talkin' complete.

"How's tricks?" says I.

"Who's your woolly friend?" the shiny Jew asks of the girls.

I looked at him a minute, but I see he'd been raised a pet, and then, too, I was so hungry for sassiety I was willin' to pass a bet or two.

"Don't you *admire* these cow gents?" snickers one of the girls.

"Play somethin', sister," says I to the one at the pianner.

She just grinned at me.

"Interdooce me," says the drummer in a kind of a way that made them all laugh a heap.

"Give us a tune," I begs, tryin' to be jolly, too.

"She don't know any pieces," says the Jew.

"Don't you?" I asks pretty sharp.

"No," says she.

"Well, I do," says I.

I walked up to her, jerked out my guns, and reached around both sides of her to the pianner. I run the muzzles up and down the keyboard two or three times, and then shot out half a dozen keys.

"That's the piece I know," says I.

But the other girl and the Jew drummer had punched the breeze.

The girl at the pianner just grinned, and pointed to the winder where they was some ragged glass hangin'. She was dead game.

"Say, Susie," says I, "you're all right, but your friends is tur'ble. I may be rough, and I ain't never been curried below the knees, but I'm better to tie to than them sons of guns."

"I believe it," says she.

So we had a drink at the bar, and started out to investigate the wonders of Cyanide.

Say, that night *was* a wonder. Susie faded after about three drinks, but I didn't seem to mind that. I hooked up to another saloon kept by a thin Dutchman. A fat Dutchman is stupid, but a thin one is all right.

In ten minutes I had more friends in Cyanide than they is fiddlers in hell. I begun to conclude Cyanide wasn't so lonesome. About four o'clock in comes a little Irishman about four foot high, with more upper lip than a muley cow, and enough red hair to make an artificial aurorer borealis. He had big red hands with freckles pasted onto them, and stiff red hairs standin' up separate and lonesome like signal stations. Also his legs was bowed.

He gets a drink at the bar, and stands back and yells:

"God bless the Irish and let the Dutch rustle!"

Now, this was none of my town, so I just stepped back of the end of the bar quick where I wouldn't stop no lead. The shootin' didn't begin.

"Probably Dutchy didn't take no note of what the locoed little dogie *did* say," thinks I to myself.

The Irishman bellied up to the bar again, and pounded on it with his fist.

"Look here!" he yells. "Listen to what I'm tellin' ye! God bless the Irish and let the Dutch rustle! Do ye hear me?"

"Sure, I hear ye," says Dutchy, and goes on swabbin' his bar with a towel.

At that my soul just grew sick. I asked the man next to me why Dutchy didn't kill the little fellow.

"Kill him!" says this man. "What for?"

"For insultin' of him, of course."

"Oh, he's drunk," says the man, as if that explained anythin'.

That settled it with me. I left that place, and went home, and it wasn't more than four o'clock, neither. No, I don't call four o'clock late. It may be a little late for night before last, but it's just the shank of the evenin' for tonight.

Well, it took me six weeks and two days to go broke. I didn't know sic 'em about minin'; and before long I *knew* that I didn't know sic 'em. Most all day I poked around them mountains—not like our'n—too much timber to be comfortable. At night I got to droppin' in at Dutchy's. He had a couple of quiet games goin', and they was one fellow among that lot of grubbin' prairie dogs that had heerd tell that cows had horns. He was the wisest of the bunch on the cattle business. So I stowed away my consolation, and made out to forget comparing Colorado with God's country.

About three times a week this Irishman I told you of—name O'Toole—comes bulgin' in. When he was sober he talked minin' high, wide, and handsome. When he was drunk he pounded both fists on the bar and yelled for action, tryin' to get Dutchy on the peck.

"God bless the Irish and let the Dutch rustle!" he yells about six times. "Say, do you hear?"

"Sure," says Dutchy, calm as a milk cow, "sure, I hears ye!"

I was plumb sorry for O'Toole. I'd like to have given him a run; but, of course, I couldn't take it up without makin' myself out a friend of this Dutchy party, and I couldn't stand for that. But I did tackle Dutchy about it one night when they wasn't nobody else there.

"Dutchy," says I, "what makes you let that bow-legged cross between a bull-dog and a flamin' red sunset tromp on you so? It looks to me like you're plumb spiritless."

Dutchy stopped wipin' glasses for a minute.

"Just you hold on," says he. "I ain't ready yet. Bimeby I make him sick; also those others who laugh with him."

He had a little gray flicker in his eye, and I thinks to myself that maybe they'd get Dutchy on the peck yet.

As I said, I went broke in just six weeks and two days. And I was broke a-plenty. No hold-outs anywhere. It was a heap long ways to cows; and I'd be teetotally chawed up and spit out if I was goin' to join these minin' terrapins defacin' the bosom of nature. It sure looked to me like hard work.

While I was figurin' what next, Dutchy came in. Which I was tur'ble surprised at that, but I said good-mornin' and would he rest his poor feet.

"You like to make some money?" he asks.

"That depends," says I, "on how easy it is."

"It is easy," says he. "I want you to buy hosses for me."

"Hosses! Sure!" I yells, jumpin' up. "You bet you! Why, hosses is where I live! What hosses do you want?"

"All hosses," says he, calm as a faro dealer.

"What?" says I. "Elucidate, my bucko. I don't take no such blanket order. Spread your cards."

"I mean just that," says he. "I want you to buy all the hosses in this camp, and in the mountains. Every one."

"Whew!" I whistles. "That's a large order. But I'm your meat."

"Come with me, then," says he. I hadn't but just got up, but I went with him to his little old poison factory. Of course, I hadn't had no breakfast; but he staked me to a Kentucky breakfast. What's a Kentucky breakfast? Why, a Kentucky breakfast is a three-pound steak, a bottle of whisky, and a setter dog. What's the dog for? Why, to eat the steak, of course.

We come to an agreement. I was to get two-fifty a head commission. So I started out. There wasn't many hosses in that country, and what there was the owners hadn't much use for unless it was to work a whim. I picked up about a hundred head quick enough, and reported to Dutchy.

"How about burros and mules?" I asks Dutchy.

"They goes," says he. "Mules same as hosses; burros four bits a head to you."

At the end of a week I had a remuda of probably two hundred animals. We kept them over the hills in some "parks," as these sots call meadows in that country. I rode into town and told Dutchy.

"Got them all?" he asks.

"All but a cross-eyed buckskin that's mean, and the bay mare that Noah bred to."

"Get them," says he.

"The bandits want too much," I explains.

"Get them anyway," says he.

I went away and got them. It was scand'lous; such prices.

When I hit Cyanide again I ran into scenes of wild excitement. The whole passel of them was on that one street of their'n, talkin' sixteen ounces to the pound. In the middle was Dutchy, drunk as a soldier—just plain foolish drunk.

"Good Lord!" thinks I to myself, "he ain't celebratin' gettin' that bunch of buzzards, is he?"

But I found he wasn't that bad. When he caught sight of me, he fell on me drivellin'.

"Look here!" he weeps, showin' me a letter.

I was the last to come in; so I kept that letter—here she is. I'll read her.

DEAR DUTCHY:—*I suppose you thought I'd flew the coop, but I haven't and this is to prove it. Pack up your outfit and hit the trail. I've made the biggest free gold strike you ever see. I'm sending you specimens. There's tons just like it, tons and tons. I got all the claims I can hold myself; but there's heaps more. I've writ to Johnny and Ed at Denver to come on. Don't give this away. Make tracks. Come in to Buck Canyon in the Whetstones and oblige.*

Yours truly,

HENRY SMITH

Somebody showed me a handful of white rock with yeller streaks in it. His eyes was bulgin' until you could have hung your hat on them. That O'Toole party was walkin' around, wettin' his lips with his tongue and swearin' soft.

"God bless the Irish and let the Dutch rustle!" says he. "And the fool had to get drunk and give it away!"

The excitement was just started, but it didn't last long. The crowd got the same notion at the same time, and it just melted. Me and Dutchy was left alone.

I went home. Pretty soon a fellow named Jimmy Tack come around a little out of breath.

"Say, you know that buckskin you bought off'n me?" says he, "I want to buy him back."

"Oh, you do," says I.

"Yes," says he. "I've got to leave town for a couple of days, and I got to have somethin' to pack."

"Wait and I'll see," says I.

Outside the door I met another fellow.

"Look here," he stops me with. "How about that bay mare I sold you? Can you call that sale off? I got to leave town for a day or two and—"

"Wait," says I. "I'll see."

By the gate was another hurryin' up.

"Oh, yes," says I when he opens his mouth. "I know all your troubles. You have to leave town for a couple of days, and you want back that lizard you sold me. Well, wait."

After that I had to quit the main street and dodge back of the hog ranch. They was all headed my way. I was as popular as a snake in a prohibition town.

I hit Dutchy's by the back door.

"Do you want to sell hosses?" I asks. "Everyone in town wants to buy."

Dutchy looked hurt.

"I wanted to keep them for the valley market," says he, "but— How much did you give Jimmy Tack for his buckskin?"

"Twenty," says I.

"Well, let him have it for eighty," says Dutchy; "and the others in proportion."

I lay back and breathed hard.

"Sell them all, but the one best hoss," says he—"no, the *two* best."

"Holy smoke!" says I, gettin' my breath. "If you mean that, Dutchy, you lend me another gun and give me a drink."

He done so, and I went back home to where the whole camp of Cyanide was waitin'.

I got up and made them a speech and told them I'd sell them hosses all right, and to come back. Then I got an Injin boy to help, and we rustled over the remuda and held them in a blind canyon. Then I called up these miners one at a time, and made bargains with them. Roar! Well, you could hear them at Denver, they tell me, and the weather reports said, "Thunder in the mountains." But it was cash on delivery, and they all paid up. They had seen that white quartz with the gold stickin' into it, and that's the same as a dose of loco to miner gents.

Why didn't I take a hoss and start first? I did think of it—for about one second. I wouldn't stay in that country then for a million dollars a minute. I was plumb sick and loathin' it, and just waitin' to make high jumps back to Arizona. So I wasn't aimin' to join this stampede, and didn't have no vivid emotions.

They got to fightin' on which should get the first hoss; so I bent my gun on them and made them draw lots. They roared some more, but done so; and as fast as each one handed over his dust or dinero he made a rush for his cabin, piled on his saddle and pack, and pulled his freight in a cloud of dust. It was sure a grand stampede, and I enjoyed it no limit.

So by sundown I was alone with the Injin. Those two hundred head brought in about twenty thousand dollars. It was heavy, but I could carry it. I was about alone in the landscape; and there were the two best hosses I had saved out for Dutchy. I was sure some tempted. But I had enough to get home on anyway; and I never yet drank behind the bar, even if I might hold up the saloon from the floor. So I grieved some inside that I was so tur'ble conscientious, shouldered the sacks, and went down to find Dutchy.

I met him headed his way, and carryin' of a sheet of paper.

"Here's your dinero," says I, dumpin' the four big sacks on the ground.

He stooped over and hefted them. Then he passed one over to me.

"What's that for?" I asks.

"For you," says he.

"My commission ain't that much," I objects.

"You've earned it," says he, "and you might have skipped with the whole wad."

"How did you know I wouldn't?" I asks.

"Well," says he, and I noted that jag of his had flew. "You see, I was behind that rock up there, and I had you covered."

I saw; and I began to feel better about bein' so tur'ble conscientious.

We walked a little ways without sayin' nothin'.

"But ain't you goin' to join the game?" I asks.

"Guess not," says he, jinglin' of his gold. "I'm satisfied."

"But if you don't get a wiggle on you, you are sure goin' to get left on those gold claims," says I.

"There ain't no gold claims," says he.

"But Henry Smith—" I cries.

"There ain't no Henry Smith," says he.

I let that soak in about six inches.

"But there's a Buck Canyon," I pleads. "Please say there's a Buck Canyon."

"Oh, yes, there's a Buck Canyon," he allows. "Nice limestone formation—make good hard water."

"Well, you're a marvel," says I.

We walked on together down to Dutchy's saloon. We stopped outside.

"Now," says he, "I'm goin' to take one of those hosses and go somewheres else. Maybe you'd better do likewise on the other."

"You bet I will," says I.

He turned around and tacked up the paper he was carryin'. It was a sign. It read:

THE DUTCH HAS RUSTLED

"Nice sentiment," says I. "It will be appreciated when the crowd comes back from that little *pasear* into Buck Canyon. But why not tack her up where the trail hits the camp? Why on this particular door?"

"Well," said Dutchy, squintin' at the sign sideways, "you see I sold this place day before yesterday—to Mike O'Toole."

The Pimienta Pancakes

by

O. HENRY

W HILE WE WERE ROUNDING UP a bunch of the Triangle-O cattle in the Frio bottoms a projecting branch of a dead mesquite caught my wooden stirrup and gave my ankle a wrench that laid me up in camp for a week.

On the third day of my compulsory idleness I crawled out near the grub wagon, and reclined helpless under the conversational fire of Judson Odom, the camp cook. Jud was a monologist by nature, whom Destiny, with customary blundering, had set in a profession wherein he was bereaved, for the greater portion of his time, of an audience.

Therefore, I was manna in the desert of Jud's obmutescence.

Betimes I was stirred by invalid longings for something to eat that did not come under the caption of "grub." I had visions of the maternal pantry "deep as first love, and wild with all regret," and then I asked:

"Jud, can you make pancakes?"

Jud laid down his six-shooter, with which he was preparing to pound an antelope steak, and stood over me in what I felt to be a menacing attitude. He further indorsed my impression that his pose was resentful by fixing upon me with his light blue eyes a look of cold suspicion.

"Say, you," he said, with candid, though not excessive, choler, "did you mean that straight, or was you trying to throw the gaff into me? Some of the boys been telling you about me and that pancake racket?"

"No, Jud," I said, sincerely, "I meant it. It seems to me I'd swap my pony and saddle for a stack of buttered brown pancakes with some first crop, open kettle, New Orleans sweetening. Was there a story about pancakes?"

Jud was mollified at once when he saw that I had not been dealing in allusions. He brought some mysterious bags and tin boxes from the grub wagon and set them in the shade of the hackberry where I lay reclined. I watched him as he began to arrange them leisurely and untie their many strings.

"No, not a story," said Jud, as he worked, "but just the logical disclosures in the case of me and that pink-eyed snoozer from Mired Mule Cañada and Miss Willella Learight. I don't mind telling you.

"I was punching then for old Bill Toomey, on the San Miguel. One day I gets all ensnared up in aspirations for to eat some canned grub that hasn't ever mooed or baaed or grunted or been in peck measures. So, I gets on my bronc and pushes the wind for Uncle Emsley Telfair's store at the Pimienta Crossing on the Nueces.

"About three in the afternoon I throwed my bridle rein over a mesquite limb and walked the last twenty yards into Uncle Emsley's store. I got up on the counter and told Uncle Emsley that the signs pointed to the devastation of the fruit crop of the world. In a minute I had a bag of crackers and a long-handled spoon, with an open can each of apricots and pineapples and cherries and greengages beside of me with Uncle Emsley busy chopping away with the hatchet at the yellow clings. I was feeling like Adam before the apple stampede, and was digging my spurs into the side of the counter and working with my twenty-four-inch spoon when I happened to look out of the window into the yard of Uncle Emsley's house, which was next to the store.

"There was a girl standing there—an imported girl with fixings on—philandering with a croquet maul and amusing herself by watching my style of encouraging the fruit canning industry.

"I slid off the counter and delivered up my shovel to Uncle Emsley.

"'That's my niece,' says he; 'Miss Willella Learight, down from Palestine on a visit. Do you want that I should make you acquainted?'

"'The Holy Land,' I says to myself, my thoughts milling some as I tried to run 'em into the corral. 'Why not? There was sure angels in Pales—Why yes, Uncle Emsley,' I says out loud, 'I'd be awful edified to meet Miss Learight.'

"So Uncle Emsley took me out in the yard and gave us each other's entitlements.

"I never was shy about women. I never could understand why some men who can break a mustang before breakfast and shave in the dark, get all left-handed and full of perspiration and excuses when they see a bolt of calico draped around what belongs in it. Inside of eight minutes me and Miss Willella was aggravating the croquet balls around as amiable as second cousins. She gave me a dig about the quantity of canned fruit I had eaten, and I got back at her, flat-footed, about how a certain lady named Eve started the fruit trouble in the first free-grass pasture—'Over in Palestine, wasn't it?' says I, as easy and pat as roping a one-year-old.

"That was how I acquired cordiality for the proximities of Miss Willella Learight; and the disposition grew larger as time passed. She was stopping at Pimienta Crossing for her health, which was very good, and for the climate, which was forty per cent hotter than Palestine. I rode over to see her once every week for a while; and then I figured it out that if I doubled the number of trips I would see her twice as often.

"One week I slipped in a third trip; and that's where the pancakes and the pink-eyed snoozer busted into the game.

"That evening, while I set on the counter with a peach and two damsons in my mouth, I asked Uncle Emsley how Miss Willella was.

"'Why,' says Uncle Emsley, 'she's gone riding with Jackson Bird, the sheep man from over at Mired Mule Cañada.'

"I swallowed the peach seed and the two damson seeds. I guess somebody held the counter by the bridle while I got off; and then I walked out straight ahead till I butted against the mesquite where my roan was tied.

"'She's gone riding,' I whisper in my bronc's ear, 'with Bird-stone Jack, the hired mule from Sheep Man's Cañada. Did you get that, old Leather-and-Gallops?'

"That bronc of mine wept, in his way. He'd been raised a cow pony and he didn't care for snoozers.

"I went back and said to Uncle Emsley: 'Did you say a sheep man?'

"'I said a sheep man,' says Uncle again. 'You must have heard tell of Jackson Bird. He's got eight sections of grazing and four thousand head of the finest Merinos south of the Arctic Circle.'

"I went out and sat on the ground in the shade of the store and leaned against a prickly pear. I sifted sand into my boots with unthinking hands while I soliloquised a quantity about this bird with the Jackson plumage to his name.

"I never had believed in harming sheep men. I see one, one day, reading a Latin grammar on hossback, and I never touched him! They never irritated me like they do most cowmen. You wouldn't go to work now, and impair and disfigure snoozers, would you, that eat on tables and wear little shoes and speak to you on subjects? I had always let 'em pass, just as you would a jackrabbit; with a polite word and a guess about the weather, but no stopping to swap canteens. I never thought it was worth while to be hostile with a snoozer. And because I'd been lenient, and let 'em live, here was one going around riding with Miss Willella Learight!

"An hour by sun they come loping back, and stopped at Uncle

Emsley's gate. The sheep person helped her off; and they stood throwing each other sentences all sprightful and sagacious for a while. And then this feathered Jackson flies up in his saddle and raises his little stewpot of a hat, and trots off in the direction of his mutton ranch. By this time I had turned the sand out of my boots and unpinned myself from the prickly pear; and by the time he gets half a mile out of Pimienta, I singlefoots up beside him on my bronc.

"I said that snoozer was pink-eyed, but he wasn't. His seeing arrangement was grey enough, but his eyelashes was pink and his hair was sandy, and that gave you the idea. Sheep man?—he wasn't more than a lamb man, anyhow—a little thing with his neck involved in a yellow silk handkerchief, and shoes tied up in bowknots.

"'Afternoon!' says I to him. 'You now ride with a equestrian who is commonly called Dead-Moral-Certainty Judson, on account of the way I shoot. When I want a stranger to know me I always introduce myself before the draw, for I never did like to shake hands with ghosts.'

"'Ah,' says he, just like that—'Ah, I'm glad to know you, Mr. Judson. I'm Jackson Bird, from over at Mired Mule Ranch.'

"Just then one of my eyes saw a roadrunner skipping down the hill with a young tarantula in his bill, and the other eye noticed a rabbit-hawk sitting on a dead limb in a water-elm. I popped over one after the other with my forty-five, just to show him. 'Two out of three,' says I. 'Birds just naturally seem to draw my fire wherever I go.'

"'Nice shooting,' says the sheep man, without a flutter. 'But don't you sometimes ever miss the third shot? Elegant fine rain that was last week for the young grass, Mr. Judson?' says he.

"'Willie,' says I, riding over close to his palfrey, 'your infatuated parents may have denounced you by the name of Jackson, but you sure moulted into a twittering Willie—let us slough off this here analysis of rain and the elements, and get down to talk that is outside the vocabulary of parrots. That is a bad habit you have got of riding with young ladies over at Pimienta. I've known birds,' says I, 'to be served on toast for less than that. Miss Willella,' says I, 'don't ever want any nest made out of sheep's wool by a tomtit of the Jacksonian branch of ornithology. Now, are you going to quit, or do you wish for to gallop up against this Dead-Moral-Certainty attachment to my name, which is good for two hyphens and at least one set of funeral obsequies?'

"Jackson Bird flushed up some, and then he laughed.

"'Why, Mr. Judson,' says he, 'you've got the wrong idea. I've called on Miss Learight a few times; but not for the purpose you imagine. My object is purely a gastronomical one.'

"I reached for my gun.

"'Any coyote,' says I, 'that would boast of dishonourable—'

"'Wait a minute,' says this Bird, 'till I explain. What would I do with a wife? If you ever saw that ranch of mine! I do my own cooking and mending. Eating—that's all the pleasure I get out of sheep raising. Mr. Judson, did you ever taste the pancakes that Miss Learight makes?'

"'Me? No,' I told him. 'I never was advised that she was up to any culinary manœuvres.'

"'They're golden sunshine,' says he, 'honey-browned by the ambrosial fires of Epicurus. I'd give two years of my life to get the recipe for making them pancakes. That's what I went to see Miss Learight for,' says Jackson Bird, 'but I haven't been able to get it from her. It's an old recipe that's been in the family for seventy-five years. They hand it down from one generation to another, but they don't give it away to outsiders. If I could get that recipe, so I could make them pancakes for myself on my ranch, I'd be a happy man,' says Bird.

"'Are you sure,' I says to him, 'that it ain't the hand that mixes the pancakes that you're after?'

"'Sure,' says Jackson. 'Miss Learight is a mighty nice girl, but I can assure you my intentions go no further than the gastro—' but he seen my hand going down to my holster and he changed his similitude—'than the desire to procure a copy of the pancake recipe,' he finishes.

"'You ain't such a bad little man,' says I, trying to be fair. 'I was thinking some of making orphans of your sheep, but I'll let you fly away this time. But you stick to pancakes,' says I, 'as close as the middle one of a stack; and don't go and mistake sentiments for syrup, or there'll be singing at your ranch, and you won't hear it.'

"'To convince you that I am sincere,' says the sheep man, 'I'll ask you to help me. Miss Learight and you being closer friends, maybe she would do for you what she wouldn't for me. If you will get me a copy of that pancake recipe, I give you my word that I'll never call upon her again.'

"'That's fair,' I says, and I shook hands with Jackson Bird. 'I'll get it for you if I can, and glad to oblige.' And he turned off down the big pear flat on the Piedra, in the direction of Mired Mule; and I steered northwest for old Bill Toomey's ranch.

"It was five days afterward when I got another chance to ride over to Pimienta. Miss Willella and me passed a gratifying evening at Uncle Emsley's. She sang some, and exasperated the piano quite a lot with quotations from the operas. I gave imitations of a rattlesnake, and told her about Snaky McFee's new way of skinning cows, and described the trip I made to Saint Louis once. We was getting along in one another's estimations fine. Thinks I, if Jackson Bird can now be persuaded to migrate, I win. I recollect his promise about the pancake receipt, and I thinks I will persuade it from Miss Willella and give it to him; and then if I catches Birdie off of Mired Mule again, I'll make him hop the twig.

"So, along about ten o'clock, I put on a wheedling smile and says to Miss Willella: 'Now, if there's anything I do like better than the sight of a red steer on green grass it's the taste of a nice hot pancake smothered in sugar-house molasses.'

"Miss Willella gives a little jump on the piano stool, and looked at me curious.

"'Yes,' says she, 'they're real nice. What did you say was the name of that street in Saint Louis, Mr. Odom, where you lost your hat?'

"'Pancake Avenue,' says I, with a wink, to show her that I was on about the family receipt, and couldn't be side-corralled off of the subject. 'Come, now, Miss Willella,' I says; 'let's hear how you make 'em. Pancakes is just whirling in my head like wagon wheels. Start her off, now—pound of flour, eight dozen eggs, and so on. How does the catalogue of constituents run?'

"'Excuse me for a moment, please,' says Miss Willella, and she gives me a quick kind of sideways look, and slides off the stool. She ambled out into the other room, and directly Uncle Emsley comes in in his shirt sleeves, with a pitcher of water. He turns around to get a glass on the table, and I see a forty-five in his hip pocket. 'Great post-holes!' thinks I, 'but here's a family thinks a heap of cooking receipts, protecting it with firearms. I've known outfits that wouldn't do that much by a family feud.'

"'Drink this here down,' says Uncle Emsley, handing me the glass of water. 'You've rid too far to-day, Jud, and got yourself over-excited. Try to think about something else now.'

"'Do you know how to make them pancakes, Uncle Emsley?' I asked.

"'Well, I'm not as apprised in the anatomy of them as some,' says Uncle Emsley, 'but I reckon you take a sifter of plaster of paris and a little dough and saleratus and corn meal, and mix 'em with eggs and buttermilk as usual. Is old Bill going to ship beeves to Kansas City again this spring, Jud?'

"That was all the pancake specifications I could get that night. I didn't wonder that Jackson Bird found it uphill work. So I dropped the subject and talked with Uncle Emsley a while about hollow-horn and cyclones. And then Miss Willella came and said 'Good-night,' and I hit the breeze for the ranch.

"About a week afterward I met Jackson Bird riding out of Pimienta as I rode in, and we stopped in the road for a few frivolous remarks.

"'Got the bill of particulars for them flapjacks yet?' I asked him.

"'Well, no,' says Jackson. 'I don't seem to have any success in getting hold of it. Did you try?'

"'I did' says I, 'and 'twas like trying to dig a prairie dog out of his hole with a peanut hull. That pancake receipt must be a jookalorum, the way they hold on to it.'

"'I'm 'most ready to give it up,' says Jackson, so discouraged in his pronunciations that I felt sorry for him; 'but I did want to know how to make them pancakes to eat on my lonely ranch,' says he. 'I lie awake at nights thinking how good they are.'

"'You keep on trying for it,' I tells him, 'and I'll do the same. One of us is bound to get a rope over its horns before long. Well, so-long, Jacksy.'

"You see, by this time we was on the peacefullest of terms. When I saw that he wasn't after Miss Willella I had more endurable contemplations of that sandy-haired snoozer. In order to help out the ambitions of his appetite I kept on trying to get that receipt from Miss Willella. But every time I would say 'pancakes' she would get sort of remote and fidgety about the eye, and try to change the subject. If I held her to it she would slide out and round up Uncle Emsley with his pitcher of water and hip-pocket howitzer.

"One day I galloped over to the store with a fine bunch of blue verbenas that I cut out of a herd of wild flowers over on Poisoned Dog Prairie. Uncle Emsley looked at 'em with one eye shut and says:

"'Haven't ye heard the news?'

"'Cattle up?' I asks.

"'Willella and Jackson Bird was married in Palestine yesterday,' says he. 'Just got a letter this morning.'

"I dropped them flowers in a cracker-barrel, and let the news trickle in my ears and down toward my upper left-hand shirt pocket until it got to my feet.

"'Would you mind saying that over again once more, Uncle Emsley?' says I. 'Maybe my hearing has got wrong, and you only said that prime heifers was 4.80 on the hoof, or something like that.'

"'Married yesterday,' says Uncle Emsley, 'and gone to Waco and Niagara Falls on a wedding tour. Why, didn't you see none of the signs all along? Jackson Bird has been courting Willella ever since that day he took her out riding.'

"'Then,' says I, in a kind of yell, 'what was all this zizzaparoola he gives me about pancakes? Tell me *that.*'

"When I said 'pancakes' Uncle Emsley sort of dodged and stepped back.

"'Somebody's been dealing me pancakes from the bottom of the deck,' I says, 'and I'll find out. I believe you know. Talk up,' says I, 'or we'll mix a panful of batter right here.'

"I slid over the counter after Uncle Emsley. He grabbed at his gun, but it was in a drawer, and he missed it two inches. I got him by the front of his shirt and shoved him in a corner.

"'Talk pancakes,' says I, 'or be made into one. Does Miss Willella make 'em?'

"'She never made one in her life and I never saw one,' says Uncle Emsley, soothing. 'Calm down now, Jud—calm down. You've got excited, and that wound in your head is contaminating your sense of intelligence. Try not to think about pancakes.'

"'Uncle Emsley,' says I, 'I'm not wounded in the head except so far as my natural cogitative instincts run to runts. Jackson Bird told me he was calling on Miss Willella for the purpose of finding out her system of producing pancakes, and he asked me to help him get the bill of lading of the ingredients. I done so, with the results as you see. Have I been sodded down with Johnson grass by a pink-eyed snoozer, or what?'

"'Slack up your grip on my dress shirt,' says Uncle Emsley, 'and I'll tell you. Yes, it looks like Jackson Bird has gone and humbugged you some. The day after he went riding with Willella he came back and told me and her to watch out for you whenever you got to talking about pancakes. He said you was in camp once where they was cooking flapjacks, and one of the fellows cut you over the head with a frying pan. Jackson said that whenever you got overhot or excited that wound hurt you and made you kind of crazy, and you went raving about pancakes. He told us to just get you worked off of the subject and soothed down, and you wouldn't be dangerous. So, me and Willella done the best by you we knew how. Well, well,' says Uncle Emsley, 'that Jackson Bird is sure a seldom kind of a snoozer.'"

During the progress of Jud's story he had been slowly but deftly combining certain portions of the contents of his sacks and cans. Toward the close of it he set before me the finished product—a pair of red-hot, rich-hued pancakes on a tin plate. From some secret hoarding place he also brought a lump of excellent butter and a bottle of golden syrup.

"How long ago did these things happen?" I asked him.

"Three years," said Jud. "They're living on the Mired Mule Ranch now. But I haven't seen either of 'em since. They say Jackson Bird was fixing his ranch up fine with rocking chairs and window curtains all the time he was putting me up the pancake tree. Oh, I got over it after a while. But the boys kept the racket up."

"Did you make these cakes by the famous recipe?" I asked.

"Didn't I tell you there wasn't no receipt?" said Jud. "The boys hollered pancakes till they got pancake hungry, and I cut this recipe out of a newspaper. How does the truck taste?"

"They're delicious," I answered. "Why don't you have some, too, Jud?"

I was sure I heard a sigh.

"Me?" said Jud. "I don't never eat 'em."

When Bob Got Throwed

by

ANONYMOUS

That time when Bob got throwed
I thought I sure would bust.
I like to died a-laffin'
To see him chewin' dust.

He crawled on that Andy bronc
And hit him with a quirt.
The next thing that he knew
He was wallowin' in the dirt.

Yes, it might a-killed him,
I heard the old ground pop;
But to see if he was injured
You bet I didn't stop.

I just rolled on the ground
And began to kick and yell;
It like to tickled me to death
To see how hard he fell.

'Twarn't more than a week ago
That I myself got throwed,
(But 'twas from a meaner horse
Than old Bob ever rode).

D'you reckon Bob looked sad and said,
"I hope that you ain't hurt!"
Naw! He just laffed and laffed and laffed
To see me chewin' dirt.

I've been prayin' ever since
For his horse to turn his pack;
And when he done it, I'd a laffed
If it had broke his back.

So I was still a-howlin'
When Bob, he got up lame;
He seen his horse had run clean off
And so for me he came.

He first chucked sand into my eyes,
With a rock he rubbed my head,
Then he twisted both my arms,—
"Now go fetch that horse," he said.

So I went and fetched him back,
But I was feelin' good all day;
For I sure enough do love to see
A feller get throwed that way.

The Moon Dance Skunk

by

A.B. GUTHRIE

T HERE WERE FIVE MEN in the back room of the Moon Dance bar—three ranchers, a hay hand and a cattle buyer—all idled by the rain that was beating outside. They had quit their pinochle game, the cards and chips lying forgotten on the green table, and were listening to old Ray Gibler who'd started on one of his stories.

Then Ray saw me and grinned and held out his big hand. "How, Tenderfoot."

"I'll listen," I said to Ray. I took off my slicker.

"I was just talking. Ought to be making tracks."

One of the ranchers said, "You ain't gonna ride herd on no dudes today."

"My woman's probably on the hunt for me."

"I'll buy a drink," I said.

Ray gave me his wide grin again. It made deep wrinkles in his leathery cheeks. "I don't like to get in the habit of refusin'."

I yelled to the bartender for a round. "What was this about a skunk?"

"Well, I'll tell you—"

Ray doodled the ice in his ditchwater highball with one horny finger . . .

It was Shorty, the sheepherder, had the skunk, and it happened right here, right in this bar, and there was rooms overhead just like now, only you boys wouldn't remember it, being still slick-eared.

Shorty was new to the town then, but it didn't take us long to find he was all sheepherder. Had a fine, steady thirst and a free hand with money. He had been herding for George I. Smith for five-six months when he decided he couldn't stand thirst nor prosperity any longer. He came to town, a sawed-off, humpy feller with a mop of black hair and a habit of talking to himself, like all herders.

He got fired up good the first day and kep' the blaze going maybe a week, while his whiskers stooled out and his clothes got dirtier and dirtier, and a man meeting him was careful to get on the wind side.

He slept all one day under the hitch rack in back of the Moon Dance Mercantile Company, and when he woke up that night he was just as dry as he was broke, which is as dry as a man can get. He tried moochin' drinks, going from one place to another, but he'd run out of credit, too, and all he got was a bad eye and good advice from the men who had his money.

I was right here, on business you might say, that night when Shorty came in and asked if the roof didn't never leak.

Whitey Hanson said, polishing a glass, "It's leaked plenty. I set 'em up for you three or four times. Git out!"

Shorty tried to argue. "My money, you got it."

"Ah-h. Why'n't you git back on the job?"

There was a couple of curly wolves in the bar, along with Whitey and Shorty and me. Anyhow, they figured they was curly. One of them was Rough Red Rourke and the other Stub Behr. Seeing Shorty, they moseyed over. "Ba-a-a," Red said in his ear, loud enough to bust an eardrum.

"Way round 'em!" Stub yelled.

Red grabbed Shorty by the shoulder. "Them pore ewes are missin' you, sweetheart."

Together they ran Shorty limp-legged through the door and pitched him in the street. Shorty got up slow, talking to himself, and dragged off.

Whitey Hanson thought that was good stuff. He said thankee to Red and Stub and poured drinks on the house.

Must have been a couple of hours later—anyhow along toward midnight—when Shorty showed up again, and not alone neither. He had a skunk with him, carrying it along by the tail so it couldn't do business. Old-timers have seen that trick worked many a time in days before saloons got to be hidyholes for spooners. Of course we didn't know the skunk was Shorty's pet.

Red saw him first and a big, drunk smile came on his face. He couldn't see the skunk on account of Shorty was carrying it on the off side. "Hey, Stub," he said, "look what I see." Then he hollered, "Ba-a-a-a!" at Shorty, so loud the roof shook.

He made for Shorty, and Shorty saw him and a look came on his face. He swung the skunk around. "By damn!" he said.

Red stopped like he'd been butted by a bull. Stub was trying to slip out of sight.

"Way round 'em!" Shorty said, and pointed the skunk and held it low, so's its front feet almost touched the floor. "Git out, both you! Git!"

He hazed them around towards the door, still holding the skunk low, business end to. It takes an awful brave man to face up to a skunk. Red and Stub wasn't that curly. They got.

Shorty closed the door after them and headed for the bar like a trout for a hopper. This was the business he had come for. He held the skunk up. To Whitey he said, "Set 'em up or I set 'im down!"

"Sure, Shorty, sure. Don't set 'im down. Nice work, Shorty." Whitey came from behind the bar and stretched his arm away out and shook Shorty's loose fist. "Them fellers couldn't buffalo you, Shorty."

Some of the rest of us ambled up, not too close, and told

Shorty he sure did shine. Shorty said, "Wasn't nothin'. Wasn't nothin'."

"It sure was, Shorty. Sure was."

I reckon all that glory was too much for Shorty. He wasn't used to compliments, but just to hearing sheep bleat and bartenders say Hell, no, they wouldn't trust him for a drink and why didn't he go to work. Yep, it must have been too much for him. Anyhow, he dropped the skunk.

Whitey jumped the counter like an antelope and tore out the back. Tubby Adams got squoze so hard in the doorway he swore his pants wouldn't fit for a month, being way big in the waist and way short in the leg. It must have taken us all of five seconds to clear out, leaving Shorty and his skunk in the saloon—with the whisky.

Well, we got together outside, still breathing hard, and held a rump session by the front door. Whitey was there, of course, and me and two or three cow hands and the printer for the *Messenger,* who was celebrating on account of getting the paper out just one day late. We couldn't see inside; Whitey always kept the shades drawn and the place dim-lit.

"Boys," Whitey said, hearing a cork pop, "we got to get him out of there."

One of the cow hands—Pete his name was, Pete Gleeson—said, "I could open the door just a crack and shoot the skunk if I had sump'n to shoot him with."

"I can't have the place stunk up," Whitey said quick. "I gotta think about my customers. I gotta think about the hotel. Ain't anyone wants to drink or sleep in a stunk-up place." He gave us an anxious look.

"I couldn't guarantee to shoot him dead first crack," the cowpoke said.

"I figure the place is already stunk up," I told Whitey.

He put his nose to the keyhole. "Maybe not. I can't smell nothin' yet. Maybe that skunk's used to Shorty." He raised his voice. "If you don't come out, Shorty, I'll have to get the law." He waited for an answer. "I'll get the sheriff."

From inside we heard Shorty holler. "Way round 'em, Shep."

"That settles it. I will get the sheriff," Whitey said. "You fellers stand guard." He moved off down the street, making for the jail.

After a while he came back, bringing Sheriff McKenzie with him. I had an idea he had been chewing McKenzie's ear off on the way.

"All right, Sheriff," Whitey said when they came up to us.

McKenzie gnawed on his mustache. "Now, Whitey, let's augur on this. What you want me to do, anyway?"

"Get Shorty and the skunk outta my place of business, that's what," Whitey told him. "And no stink!"

"It's a big order, Whitey, a mighty big order," the sheriff said.

Whitey never did like the sheriff much. "The taxes I pay, looks like you would have an idea."

"Your paying taxes don't seem to help me much right now."

"You got a reputation as a fast man with a gun. Anyhow, you used to have. But watch you don't hit my new mirror."

McKenzie chewed his whiskers some more. "I don't know. I wouldn't say I was *that* fast."

Tubby Adams said, "Try persuadin'. Looks like Shorty would feel plumb agreeable by now."

The sheriff walked up to the door. "This here's the law, Shorty. This here's the sheriff. You gotta come outta there, Shorty. Best come peaceful. Best not make a stink."

What he got back was a song, or a piece of it. It sounded real pretty there in the dark.

"He's a killer and a hater!
He's the great annihilator!
He's a terror of the boundless prairie."

"Don't look like I'm doin' any good,'" McKenzie said, turning around to us. He tried it again. "I don't want no trouble, Shorty. You gonna make me come in and git you?"

This time Shorty answered, "Yah."

The sheriff backed away. "This is serious, sure enough."

He kept bitin' his whiskers and got an idea. "We'll just throw open the door and let the skunk come out by hisself."

We all looked at each other. It wasn't for nothin' we had put McKenzie in the sheriff's office, you bet. McKenzie put his hand on the knob while the rest of us got ready to light out. Only the knob wouldn't turn. Shorty wasn't as dumb as you might think.

"You get any smell?" Whitey asked.

MacKenzie put his snout to the keyhole. "Yep."

"Oh, hell!"

"Rotgut," the sheriff said. "The stink of plain rotgut. Nothin' else. Reckon that skunk's ashamed of his equipment by comparison."

Tubby hitched his pants. "Long as you won't let anybody shoot that woods pussy, ain't nothin' to do but starve Shorty out."

"Starve 'im out!" Whitey bawled. "Starve him out, you damn fool! You think he'll want to eat?"

"I hadn't give proper thought to that," Tubby answered.

The printer swallowed another hiccup. "Have to wait till the well runs dry."

Whitey clapped his hands to his head.

"I could use a drink myself," the sheriff put in.

Come to think of it, all of us could. From here on we began to think deep.

I called the boys away from the door so's Shorty couldn't hear. "Ain't there a way to poison skunks? What they eat, anyhow?"

"Chickens," Tubby answered. "Damn 'em!"

"I hear tell they eat frogs and snakes," the printer said.

While we were thinking frogs and snakes, Shorty began on another tune.

"Drink that rotgut, drink that rotgut,
Drink that redeye, boys;
It don't make a damn wherever we land,
We hit her up for joy."

"A frog now," Tubby said while he scratched his head with one hand. "Or snakes. Then there's the poison."

"I guess it ain't no trouble for you to put your hand on a frog or snake any old time," Whitey said.

"My boy's got himself a collection. I don't figger he'd mind partin' with a frog or a snake." Tubby licked his mouth. "Not in a good cause, anyway."

"It might work," the printer said. "Worth tryin'."

So Tubby said he'd get a frog, and Pete Gleeson—that was the cow hand—said he'd rout the druggist out and get some strychnine.

By and by they came back, Tubby holding a little old frog that was still mostly tadpole and Pete bringing powdered strychnine in a paper bag.

"First," said Sheriff McKenzie, taking charge of things, "we got to poison the frog. Pry his mouth open, one of you."

We gave the frog a good pinch of poison, with a drop of water for a chaser, and nosed him up to the crack and tried to goose him in. No go. That frog wouldn't budge.

After a while we found out it was because he was dead already.

"The frog idea ain't so good," the sheriff said. "Even with a live frog, it wouldn't work. A frog moves by hoppin'. How's he gonna hop *under* a door? Just bump his head, is all. Sump'n quick and slithery would be the ticket, like a snake."

"And don't poison him inside," I said. "Poison him out."

"'Nother thing," Pete Cleeson put in. "Roll 'im in something sticky first, like flypaper."

You can see we was all thinkin' dry and hard.

Tubby went back to the house and got a garter snake, and Pete waked the druggist up again to get a sheet of flypaper. The druggist came along with him this time, figuring it wasn't any use to try to sleep.

Tubby and the sheriff didn't mind handlin' the snake.

The strychnine clung fine to the flypaper stickum, and the stickum clung fine to the snake. You never saw a snake like that one! All powdered up pretty, with a kind of a flounce around the neck where the strychnine was extra thick. You would have thought it was going to a wedding.

It could still crawl, though. Tubby pointed it at the crack and let go, and it slipped inside slick as butter.

Shorty was singing "Red Wing" now, only you could tell he had already sung his best and didn't have much class left in him.

"How long," asked Whitey, "does it take strychnine to work?"

The druggist chewed the question over with himself and came out with, "Depends."

"We'll give 'er plenty of time," Whitey said. "I won't open the place till mornin'."

"We done a lot of thinkin' for you," Tubby said, looking at Whitey sad-eyed. "Got a frog, too, and a snake."

"All right. All right, I'll set 'em up in the morning." Whitey talked as if it hurt him.

So we all dragged away, figuring, of course, to be on deck come opening time, which we were.

Whitey had the sheriff with him again, and there was all the rest of us, plus quite a crowd who'd heard about the doings.

"Might have to break the door down," Whitey said. "I can't unlock her if she's locked from inside." He turned to McKenzie. "Sheriff, do your duty."

The sheriff waited a while, as if to show he wasn't taking orders from the likes of Whitey. Then he up and turns the knob and the door swung open.

It was just like we'd left it, the place was, except for a couple of empty bottles. No Shorty. No skunk. No snake. No nothing. It was just like we'd left it, except Whitey's new mirror was busted all to hell, which made us feel awful sorry for him. Business took up as usual.

Ray drained his glass. "I was tellin' the boys before you came in it was a stinkless skunk. Been separated from his ammunition, you might say, though we didn't know it, of course. The place didn't smell a bit worse than it does now."

"You mean the skunk ate the snake and went off and died, and so Shorty left?" I asked.

"Oh, no. That wasn't the way of it at all. What happened was we cured Shorty. He had picked up his skunk and lit out. Never touched a drop afterwards. He said he'd seen snakes plenty of times while drinkin', but by grab when he saw one with frostin' on it, it was time to quit."

Ol Antoine's Wooden Overcoat

by

PAUL ST. PIERRE

THE NEWS OF OL ANTOINE'S DEATH came to the Namko Country at the end of a soft summer day and interrupted the celebration of a famous victory by Namko's Cattlemen's Association. Death and glory commonly come together, the one factual, the other no more than an exhalation of the human spirit and intangible as the breath of God. But in Namko a familiar epic of mankind could be played out in a fashion not known elsewhere. In Namko, death and the glory were dissociated, one from the other. They began as no more than coincidence. They became enmeshed only because nature so often imitates art.

As for the glorious victory, it was, by global standards, a small one, suitable to the rural poor. It involved a new federal/provincial program for public uplift called the Agricultural and Rural Development Act. Here and there across the land, it had succeeded in draining a swamp or two.

In that year Namko's entire economy was a swamp. The winter had been cold beyond any where the memory of man runs. Spring had come one step forward two steps back, so that for much of it the country was glazed in ice. Neither cows nor horses could rustle through the crust and those that had exhausted the hay stacks starved. Even the moose, weakened by hunger and cold, began dying during that long and reluctant spring. The new sun nourished only the ticks in their fur. When Smith moved his horses to his Spring Turnout, a valley bottom where the new grass first appeared each year, he took five days for a two-day drive because they were too weak for more than a lank, slow shuffle and some kept falling. "It wasn't a drive," he said. "It was more like escorting some old ladies across a street. To the hospital."

In that year the price of beef fell, the price of furs fell and taxes, as ever, rose.

Hunger, despair and death were shared by all, men and animals. The story of their collective miseries coursed back and forth across the wide plateau.

In a valley not far from the Namko ranges, one of Chilcotin's better men did not winter in that year. He was a quiet, gentle soul who, ranching two hundred head of breeding stock, had been able for five years to pay board for a mongoloid daughter in a Vancouver nursing home. In that winter, broke, he had to bring her home. By Christmas, he was no longer able to endure what he perceived to be the reproach of her pale and vacant eyes, so he poked his 30-30 into his mouth and blew his head away.

Some echo of this anguish reached the great world outside the realms of the cattlemen and there was a vague public sentiment that help should be rendered them. The help, naturally enough, did not materialize until the following summer.

By that time there was lots of grass, lots of hay and more than one rancher had forgotten how cold and hungry he had been a few months before. However when help did come it was of a spectacular nature, so much so that a special summer meeting of the Cattlemen's Association was invoked to hear an announcement by the government men.

There, without preliminary discussion, without time to consider and without having asked for anything, they were informed that

Namko was to become an ARDA district. There would be a major range improvement program, the draining of wet meadows and the irrigation of dry ones by damming creeks. They would be employed by their governments to do this work, on their own lands, at staggering hourly rates of pay. Being unblessed by any form of local government, they would be required to make no contribution of any kind to the great project. The entire capital cost, half a million dollars no less, would be borne by the federal and provincial governments.

This boon was purveyed to them by a bureaucrat of the mandarin class. It was his misfortune to enjoy a good salary, lifetime tenure and the prospect of a pension larger than he could hope to spend. He therefore had very little understanding of such things as cold, hunger and other troubles of the vulgar sort, and when he rose to speak before the assembled ranchers his manner was that of God letting the fish have water.

He and the clutch of officials who had accompanied him experienced a sudden education. The ranchers responded gravely, softly, even courteously but in a manner totally unexpected. In less than an hour they had publicly debated, found themselves to be of a common mind and voted. They voted an absolute and unequivocal rejection of the offer on the principle that governments knew bugger-all about ranching and were best kept far away from where anything worthwhile was to be done.

"The wages and the investment and the range improvements sound nice," as Larsen put it, "but if we once let government start messing around with our business we will never get rid of the bastards."

To men of the nation's new ruling class, the churlishness of such peasants was beyond comprehension. They tried, politely as they thought, to suggest that such ingratitude was unseemly, but the ranchers retreated into a glassy silence. Despairing, the government men fled in their rented four-wheel drive station wagons, the sleek and shiny vehicles glinting in the sun as they rustled over the narrow, twisting and humped little Namko trail, flying like a wisp of teal which had been shot at and narrowly missed.

The ranchers remained, deeply satisfied with whatever it was they had accomplished. The whole matter had come to them unbidden and had been disposed of by instinct rather than by rational thought, but they were conscious, nevertheless, that they had nailed a flag to a mast while the cannon shot flew thickly about their ears.

Suffused in the rich brew of righteousness, which was further enriched in that their wives were berating them for their decision, they decided to tarry a day at the centre of Namko. Abandoning all the duties of riding, haying and fence building they threw up a little tent city beside the small river. The women found food and fry pans, the men found whisky, both familiar miracles at such times. The women raised tents, sent their children for water and cooked. The men sat around, drank whisky and talked about things that really mattered. Darkness pooled in the bottom of the shallow valley, filled it and crept up over the hills to overwhelm the red fire of a long sunset as the stars, one by one, came out to watch over the campfires. It was at times like these that they knew they were blessed among all men.

There was nothing in the manner of Young Alexander's arrival in the camp which gave warning of the news about Ol Antoine. Young Alexander, who was old enough that most men had forgotten who the Old Alexander was, was a frequent visitor at the ranch houses. He had cowboyed across most of the country for twenty years or more and still hired out occasionally in the pleasanter months of summer and autumn. He lived apart from the Reserve, keeping a tent and a couple of horses on the Behind Meadow most of the year and retreating to the cabin of one or another relative on the Reserve only in the bitterest weather of winter.

The men at the fire heard the tap of his horse's feet on the dirt road, looked into the black shadows under the pines and watched the shape of the horse emerge from among the trees. When the rider was close enough that they could hear the creak of his saddle, Young Alexander spoke. "Hello this place."

"It's Young Alexander, en't it?" said Larsen.

Young Alexander did not answer.

He dismounted at a tree fifteen feet from the fire, dallied the lines loosely on the saddle horn, tied a halter rope long enough to allow the animal to feed at its feet and walked over to where the three men sat on a deadfall log.

"We just ate, but there's more," said Larsen. Although the Indian did not answer his silence was consent. "Got some more grub, Margaret?"

Margaret Larsen emerged from the lean-to and began to rustle meat for frying and a pan to do it in.

"Here, Alec," said Morton, producing a bottle, "something that will make a better rancher out of you."

Morton and Alec had a drink together the odd time.

They had developed a ritual for this, and in that country rituals were cherished, particularly homemade ones. Morton would pass the bottle, holding it at the heel and Alec would grasp it with an exaggerated firmness—a recognition that Morton had been in the country long enough to have become familiar with the ancient Indian style of saying thank you.

Instead of grasping the bottle in the usual style, Young Alexander held his hand out, palm forward.

"What's got into you," said Morton.

Young Alexander sat on the log, crossed his arms on his knees and looked at the flames.

"Well have some coffee while you're waiting for grub," said Larsen. He poured a cup from the billycan.

The man took it and drank. He would, they knew, talk when he was ready. If he did not, it meant that he had nothing to say, and that, too, should be a man's privilege.

He spoke just before the other three were about to pick up the thread of a conversation they had dropped.

"I guess you don't hear about that thing on the Reserve," he said.

"Ain't none of us been over there today, I don't think," said Larsen.

"Not so good," said Young Alexander.

He rolled a cigarette and lit it.

"Peoples feel bad," he said. He paused again. "Ol Antoine, he's dead in that place Williams Lek."

"Well I'll be a go to hell," said Larsen.

"You maybe got it wrong," said Smith. "Ol Antoine wasn't sick. He just went to hospital to have them look at his eyes. New glasses or something."

"That's all it is," said the Indian. "But he gets in that place and he dies."

"I'll be damned," said Smith. "You know, he had talked about dying for so long I figured he was never gonna do it, that he was gonna talk it out instead."

"Same like us," said Young Alexander. "We figure there's always gonna be an Ol Antoine this place. We all got to think that way."

"The closest thing to a national monument we ever had in Namko I guess," said Morton. He produced a bottle again. "Come on. Let's all have a drink to him. He was a good old man."

This time Young Alexander joined as they drank, passing the bottle hand to hand.

"Well look at it this way," said Larsen. "There is no reason people should feel bad. He lived a long time and I guess he went quick and easy. People don't have to feel bad about that, Alec."

"It's not same thing. The peoples feel bad because they bury Ol Antoine at Williams Lek."

"He's buried already!"

"No. Not now. Little time, pretty soon, they bury him at Williams Lek."

Through Margaret, who had been standing within earshot, the news spread around the half dozen camps on the flat beside the river and others came up to the fire. There was general discussion which was slow and often confusing. Young Alexander was known as a man who said very little in Chilcotin and English came a poor second, devoid of tense and sometimes of sense. The story was slow in taking final shape, as had been the Indian and his horse emerging from the darkness, but in time it fleshed out and was tangible and clear. Ol Antoine was to go to a pauper's grave in Williams Lake Cemetery.

The story delivered, Young Alexander departed with his horse, carrying his message to others of the Namko band who, this night, would be camped on meadows where they were cutting hay on contract.

"Potters' field for that old man," said Morton. "What do you think of that?"

"I don't know that it makes much difference once you're dead," said Smith. "But of course I have never been much for funerals. Your funeral is just where people who never knew you give you a bunch of flowers that you can't smell."

"But it does make a difference," said Frenchie, who had now joined them. "I guess the band would feel bad. I'd feel bad."

"Damn right," said Larsen. "He should be buried here on the Reserve."

"Yes," said his wife, "along with all the others. Two sticks nailed together for a cross and his name written in pencil on the wood."

"You got that tone in your voice," said Larsen to her.

"When were any of you last in that graveyard?" she said. "There's a pine box a few feet down in the gravel and on top there's just what I said. Sticks with pencil writing on them and the marks bleach out in the sun and soon the only identification of who lies down there is in the mind of somebody who's still alive up here."

"That ain't our fault," he said.

"It's somebody's fault," she said. "When some people have so much in this world and some have so little."

"Alright then," said Smith. "Why can't the Cattlemen's Association bring him back to be buried here?"

"Yes, and get him a good coffin too," said Morton.

The electricity of that heady afternoon meeting had not left them. Instinctively, like a school of fish, they turned to face in a single direction and swam with the purpose lent by powerful instinct. It had always been their style. When they chose not to do something, neither glory, gold nor choirs of angels could move them, either singly or collectively. But on the rare occasion when they were seized with a common purpose they would go through the fire and ice of Norwegian hell to achieve it.

There ensued a series of abrupt command decisions of considerable tactical skill.

Stettler, who was known as a good tracker, was sent to trail Young Alexander through the pines and retrieve him to the camp.

Two men were dispatched to the Namko Hotel and Store and told to summon Arch MacGregor, Honorary Treasurer of the Cattlemen's Association. He was a man often hard to shift but they were instructed to use force if necessary.

Some other Indians from the Reserve had now made their way into the camp and when Larsen declared a formal session of the Cattlemen's Association to be in session they were tacitly included as members pro tem.

Larsen, standing on the tailgate of his pickup truck, presided over the second meeting of that day and it was, like the first, extraordinary for the speed with which it was conducted and the lack of talk involved.

It was moved, seconded and approved by vote that Smith, in company with Young Alexander, would drive Larsen's truck to Williams Lake for the body of Ol Antoine, leaving before the dawn.

Another motion required that Herb, the sometime local mechanic, be snatched from his bed and taken to his log garage near the hotel, there to install by the light of gas lanterns a needed oil gasket in Larsen's truck. It was recognized that force would be needed in this case to overcome Herb's natural misanthropy and laziness but the posse was told not to use it excessively. "Break his arm and he'll be no good for monkey wrenching anyhow," as Morton observed.

There would be a wake for Ol Antoine, and the community's single phone line, if it could be roused from its silence, would be used by a phone committee to alert the rest of Chilcotin to this event.

Since the salmon were running in the big river twenty miles distant, the main fare would be Chilcotin turkey. Three men were to be dispatched at dawn to dipnet them, two to use the net and one to stand on a nearby hill and watch for a game warden. The Indians would barbecue the turkeys.

Norah and Margaret were to cook bread and dried apricot pies and other foods.

Henry James was to ride, leading a spare saddle horse, across the mountain to fetch the Oblate priest, Father Fitzjames, who was known to be visiting an off-road reserve there.

There were to be drums, dancing and a LaHelle game at the wake and children were to be detailed to collect masses of wild roses to lay upon the grave.

"As for the price of the coffin, we will use the Cattlemen's Association surplus for it. So moved? Moved. Seconded? Seconded. All in favor? Motion passed. We do have enough, do we Arch?"

"Hell yes," said Arch.

"How much is it?"

Arch pulled a paper from his shirt and read from it. "The surplus as of today is one thousand, two hundred and forty-seven dollars and fifty-three cents."

Larsen almost lost his balance on the tailgate.

"Did you say twelve hundred? Twelve hundred dollars!"

Arch read the figures again.

"Impossible," said Smith.

"I thought it was about three hundred dollars," said Larsen.

"You forget," said Arch, "you guys were your own bootleggers at this year's Stampede. You brought a bunch of booze in on the stage and I sold it to you a bottle at a time."

"But that was to be at cost," said Larsen.

"At cost plus one percent for handling," said Arch.

"And at one percent it amounted to a thousand dollars?"

"One percent profit," said Arch. "Buy for one dollar, sell for two dollars. One percent."

Silence overtook them all. Men scratched their back hair, peered at their boots, clutched their belt buckles. It had indeed been a day of shock and surprise. Finally all the faces, the white and the brown, turned toward Larsen. They did not speak to him. They looked at him. They granted him the lonely weight of command.

He may have remembered the rift in the ranks of the association a few years previously when an entire afternoon had been spent debating the unauthorized spending of twenty-five dollars on a new gate at the stampede grounds, a bitter battle which had ended in Frenchie resigning the presidency. But the past is not master of the present and Larsen trusted to instinct, which prompted him well.

"Well that's good," he said. "Smith, you got enough to buy a good one."

"That's what we voted," said Morton.

"If necessary, spend it all," said Larsen. "Just be sure you get one with some style."

"Something that measures up to the dignity of the Namko Cattlemen's Association," said Smith.

"Agreed," they all said.

Later, the meeting ending and the crowd dispersing, Morton

drew Larsen aside and said, "Imagine, the government offering us money when we had all that of our own."

"There is no understanding governments," Larsen said.

By dawn, Herb had infused some new life and vigor into Larsen's truck, although it still spit clear blue smoke from the exhaust. Also the shocks had given up, the engine sounded like a bagful of hammers and steering it, as Smith said, was like leading a poodle on a leash.

With a dedication unusual of him he ground steadily east into Williams Lake, pausing not to visit and stopping not to talk for he knew that it was in such practices that the gods stole time from mankind. When sleepiness overtook him near the Sheep Creek Hill switchbacks, he rolled the truck into the pines and he and Young Alexander slept a few hours, crouched in the cab.

They rumbled into the Lake at 3 A.M. Smith left Young Alexander at the Holding Grounds above the town. He might sleep some more there and in the morning, make his way into the town and begin, even if not complete, the process of claiming Ol Antoine's body.

Smith drove north to Prince George, a town which served as bellybutton for the province of British Columbia. Prince had been no more than a fur-trade post for most of its life, but the Pacific Great Eastern Railway had now, after more than a quarter of a century of political convulsions, crept into the place and met the Canadian National Railway line. Lumber and pulp mills were being built and the main street had stores with large plate-glass windows and such exotic stock as lawn mowers, plate-glass coffee tables, wall-to-wall carpeting—all the stuff of the new prosperity in the great national suburbia. Smith was unshaven, the crotch of his jeans was torn and he was dirtier than six pet coons. As so often in these places, he felt alien and unwanted.

Having ten dollars of his own, he decided to spend five of them on a new shirt. It might, he felt, offset the torn jeans. The first clothing store he encountered was a new one, built to look like an old English one, and the clerk, who aspired to old English ways, enquired, "What is your pleasure, sir?"

"Fucking and shooting pheasants," said Smith. "But what I came here for was to buy a shirt."

The conversation was all downhill from that point, but Smith walked out wearing a new shirt. He sensed, however, that it wasn't doing much for him. He was still dirty, and had enough smell under his armpits to knock a dog off a gutwagon.

Matters went no better at the undertaking parlor. There were, Smith observed, a lot of soft-handed people with expensive clothes in this country now.

"An Indian?" said the salesman. "You don't have to buy coffins for Indians. The Indian Department supplies them."

Smith had been doing his best to try to forget that fact, so it enraged him to hear it from a stranger. He did not, however, let that emotion out where it could be seen and shot at, but spoke mildly. "In our country we take care of our own people," he said.

He was wandering through the display and paused beside a box of shining oak and satin. "What's this one?"

"It's excellent. One of the best."

"I mean, how much?"

"It's five hundred dollars."

This, by coincidence, was what Smith had paid two years before to buy a hay meadow. He had borrowed from the bank for it and had been two years in the repayment.

He fingered the satin.

"I dunno," he said, "there's something kind of sleazy about it."

He moved on, tapping wood, fingering bronze handles and expressing vague dissatisfaction until he reached the one which he had spotted the first moment he entered the showroom. "Now that," he said, "is as good a wooden overcoat as I've seen in your place."

"It's twelve hundred dollars."

"Well now, it just might be worth that. Silver handles?"

"Silver handles, Philippine mahogany and pure silk. I'm sorry sir, it's taken."

"Taken, you say. Now that's a pity."

"You may have heard that Arvid Green has passed on."

"I have heard of Arvid Green," said Smith. All the country had heard of Mr. Green. When middle-aged, he had made a million dollars in real estate speculation during the Grand Trunk construction boom. He had devoted the rest of his life to preventing fellow citizens from taking a nickel of it away from him. "He's rich, ain't he?" said Smith.

"He was very well-to-do. I'm expecting the family this morning."

"Expecting them? I thought they had already bought it."

"They will buy it, you can be assured."

"You mean, there is nothing signed? No down payment?"

"No. There is, as you put it, no down payment from the estate."

"Then as I understand the law, it is for sale," said Smith. He reached into his hip pocket. He had been supplied the association's surplus in cash, from Arch MacGregor's tin strongbox, a thick mound of twenties and an occasional fifty. "We'll take it," he said.

"Is this some kind of joke?"

Smith kept counting, licking his fingers to separate old bills that stuck. "The guy who died didn't think so. Here, you can count it. Twelve hundred. I'll come around for it in an hour and rope it on the back of the pickup."

He left the mound of money on the stand where the king of all wooden overcoats stood. He started to the door, pausing only to turn and say, in the gentlest of tones, "When Arvid Green's people come in, you can tell them that this coffin was bought by the Namko Cattlemen's Association. The Namko Cattlemen's Association. Tell them we had an old Indian we needed to bury."

If the others, Smith thought, were doing their jobs as well as he was, there was going to be a first-class funeral in Namko.

Oddly enough, others were. Frequently in Namko elaborate community plans were erected which collapsed almost as quickly. People forgot their tasks or did the wrong ones twice, or the participants began to bicker among themselves. In the funeral of Ol Antoine, there was to be none of that disarray.

By the evening of the day following Smith's departure the grave had been dug by Indians at the Reserve and a sturdy wooden cross made with Ol Antoine's name carved deep in the yellow pine, so deep that wind, sun and weather might not erase it for a century or more.

The catching of the salmon was proceeding. Henry James had shot a small doe deer and this meat was being given a fast, hard smoke at Frenchie's smokehouse. Mountains of bread and cakes were being baked. There would be food for all.

On the Reserve, where poverty had been general and complete for years, the people were making the same discovery—that there are always riches to be found when giving is required. Stocks of smoked trout emerged. So did many gallon jars of sopallillie, which would give a touch of grandeur to the eating. Sopallillie, made from berries, was a dark, frothy concoction, nonalcoholic, astringent and unique. As with blue cheese, oolichan oil and sometimes sex, people had to acquire a taste for sopallillie, but to those who had—most of the Indians and a few of the old-timers among the whites—it occupied a reserved space in the territory of heaven.

Father Fitzjames had been found in the remote camp to the north and was riding back to Namko across the mountains.

"At this rate," said Arch MacGregor, "not only is the funeral going to be held on the day we said, it is going to go off at the hour we said."

"Do not speak well of the day until the sun has set," said Frenchie's Wife.

"What could go wrong?" said Frenchie.

She did not answer.

What could go wrong went wrong twenty thousand feet above their heads.

As happened from time to time during Chilcotin summers, there had been a pooling of hot, moist air on the land behind the Coast Range. It made for a sticky heat, but pleasant scenery. For days, each noon saw small and innocent puffs of cumulus clouds forming to give some pattern to a sky which would otherwise have been a solid stretch of uninteresting blue.

On the third day, all this was in convulsions. Out of the Pacific, impelled by the whimsical forces which meteorologists can never fully comprehend, a flow of cold air from the Alaskan Coast turned sharply east and drove across the crests of the Coast Range. So rapidly did it move that the cold air rode over the top of the warm, moist air in Chilcotin. Just east of the range, the system stalled. The result was a cauldron. Cold, heavy air plunged earthward; moist, warm air burst upward. The sky turned black. Fierce and erratic winds broke trees and flattened haystacks. Thunderhead clouds rose twenty-five and thirty thousand feet into the far skies. Hail as large as hens' eggs pounded the ground and then rains came, an inch an hour and more, such rain as the land had not seen for a year, five years, maybe more. Morton Dilloughboy was to later testify that in that rain he had to hold his pipe in his mouth upside down that he did not drown.

The single phone line to Williams Lake went down, a full half mile of it, together with the score of trees to which it was nailed. This did not much matter, since the lines had been dead for days from causes unknown. It did, however, ensure that days more would elapse before Namko might again speak to an uncaring world outside.

By noon on the day set for the funeral, when Smith had been expected to arrive, all creeks had risen dangerously and one a few miles from Namko, called the Lettergo Gallagher, was tearing at the foundations of its bridge.

Alarmed by reports that the one bridge on the road might go out, Larsen led a party of men to it. If there was one place where Smith might be stopped by such a storm, the Lettergo it seemed to be.

The storm was leaving and making its way eastward as they arrived. The hammer of the rain stopped beating, the winds turned playful. But the Lettergo continued to rise.

The bridge, a few stout logs bound by cables and crossed by thick planks, stood well above the boil of the water but each end rested on only a flimsy fretwork of log cribbing. When they arrived, the cribbing had begun to break loose. Within half an hour it was gone and so was the gravel bank and the end of the little bridge dropped into the creek which frothed white against it and, plank by plank, ate it for breakfast. Sodden, their clothes now steaming in the rapidly drying air, the little band solemnly watched it go.

"We could of saved it if we had a tractor," said Frenchie.

"And if we'd packed a ham sandwich, we could call it a picnic," said Morton. "What the hell's the use of talking about tractors."

"All is well," said Larsen, whose lips and hands were blue and body shivering. "We will ferry Smith and the coffin across it."

"A boat will go half a mile downstream in that current," said Morton.

"So will we, to meet it," said Larsen.

"I don't think Smith he likes water much," said Jim Dan.

"He will have to learn to like it today, fast," said Larsen.

Jim Dan was given a truck and sent back to the Reserve for a rowboat. The ferry party waited, warming themselves at a bonfire and speculating on how many fallen trees might lie on the Chilcotin road beyond their vision, trees which Smith would have to beavertail his way through with the dull axe stowed in the Larsen truck.

Jim Dan came back without the boat.

"He ain't here, Smith," said Jim.

"We know goddam well he ain't here," said Larsen. "Where is the boat?"

"I said he ain't here," said the Indian.

"Shut up a minute, Ken," said Morton. "Jim. Where is he? Smith."

Jim pointed to a meadow they could not see through the trees. "My kid, he's riding saddle horse, he finds Smith on Wild Horse Meadow. He's stuck that place."

"He's taken Old Road," said Larsen. "Why in hell would he go that way?"

"Why would he come this way," said Morton, "to a washed-out bridge."

"How could he know it was washed out?"

"Let's go see him. We can ask."

Larsen swore again and kicked the fire with his boots, driving sparks and flames about them.

"If he's on the Wild Horse, he must of forded the creek before she boiled up," said Morton.

When Larsen did not reply he continued, "Ken, don't get sore because you can't have your own particular kind of rescue operation. You just got your mind too set on this ferry boat operation. We will get him out of Wild Horse instead of fishing him and the coffin out of this creek. One way is as good as another."

"I s'pose you're right. Okay. We will hike it, cross-country, and push him out."

"Might be best s'pose we take this truck," said Jim.

"And stick two trucks instead of one? There is hardly anything left of Old Road and what there is will be all blowdowns today." Larsen, resuming the command he had almost relinquished, spoke with the firmness natural to generals. "We walk it, I say, and push him. Jim here could push him out all by himself if he had to. The rest of us could just stand and watch him."

Jim smiled. "Hiyu push, I think maybe," he said. He was a big man, two yards high, two hundred and twenty-five pounds of steely bones and rippling muscles. People in the Namko Country were grateful that he had been born good-natured.

"Hiyu walk," said Morton.

They walked to Old Road. Old Road had been cut by the storekeeper who preceded Arch at Namko. In 1935, claiming the distinction of the first man to drive a gas powered vehicle to Namko, he had cut a strange trail through the meadows and forests of the western plateau. Traveling by winter, when swamps were frozen, he had brought the machine through by following a series of meadows and hacking out trees in the intervening arms of forest. For several years, he and other men of Namko had tried to make this an all year truck road, but they could never be more than mildly successful because most of the meadows were soft ground. In the forties Old Road had been abandoned to horses, wagons and cattle drives and they had cut the present road along the jack-pine ridges where the base was rocky.

The party made its way slowly, unwillingly, through the pines. None of them were men who fancied walking, holding firm to the belief that walking had been unnecessary since the taming of horses some centuries before. Walking was a low pursuit, fitted only to trappers, prospectors and Englishmen.

The sun broke through as they reached the Wild Horse Meadow and illuminated the steaming yellow grass, the truck and the figure of Smith, who was sitting on the tailgate, smoking a cigarette. A deceptively placid scene, it worsened as the rescue party drew nearer. The truck sat low, its belly to the grass. Two lines of grey mud, hubcap deep, were traced behind the wheels but to the front there was none. Smith was in the loonshit.

Loonshit was a gumbo; it was undetectable when dry but when thoroughly soaked in water a patch of it took on the character of molasses mixed with glue. All men encountered loonshit sooner or later in that country and all but the strongest wept when they did.

So came the six of them to the silent Smith, the battered, dirty old truck and the grey slime. They stood silently beside it. Frenchie was the first to speak.

"Beautiful," he said. "Absolutely beautiful."

"It is a dandy," said Morton.

And Larsen agreed that Smith could not have done better. They were looking at the coffin, wedged and bound between two bales of hay.

"Philippine mahogany," said Smith. "The heartwood. That's why it's so red. The old man is gonna go in style."

"You couldn't have done better," said Larsen.

"The handles," said Smith, "you can't see them, but the handles are solid silver."

It was some time before their thoughts turned to the matter of saving the truck.

"How did you get her in a mess like that Smith?" said Larsen.

"To hell with you and the horse you rode in on," said Smith amiably.

"What I want to know is, why did you try this road?"

"I told you," said Morton, "he knew the bridge was out. He's got a sixth sense, Smith."

"That's right," said Smith.

"BS," said Larsen. "You never knew the bridge was out. Why this way?"

"Young Alexander's camp is just up that way. He wanted to get a change of clothes and his horse."

"You're a lunatic," said Larsen.

"I forded the creek, didn't I?"

"Alright. Alright. We will get her out. Although how we pick our way into Namko God only knows."

Smith rose and stretched. "All is well," he said.

"All is not well," said Larsen. "The funeral is pretty soon. What time is it, anyway?"

Nobody had brought a watch. They studied the sun and guessed. They guessed they would be late.

"Hell of a note," said Larsen. "Everybody waiting on us."

"Don't worry," said Smith, "only thing a man has got to worry about in this world is does he go to heaven or does he go to hell."

"Right," shouted Morton, who knew and liked the story. "If he goes to heaven he's got nothing to worry about and if he goes to hell he is so busy snatching sparks out of his ass and shaking hands with all his old friends he ain't got time to worry."

For an hour, they did not have time to worry.

They first rocked the truck, Smith playing gears from forward to reverse with six men pushing. The truck settled deeper and Smith pronounced her firmly high centred and maybe there for the winter. Larsen berated him as defeatist.

They dragged deadfall from the edge of the meadow, jacked the truck high and stuffed the slim logs beneath the wheels. The truck slipped off and spun its wheels again in the loonshit.

All except Smith, who retained his position as truck driver, were caked in mud from elbow to breakfast time. Tempers shortened. At one point Henry James suggested that they remove the coffin to dry grass, lest it be dirtied, and climbed to the back of the truck to loosen ropes. Frenchie leapt like a hungry trout and struck down his arms. "Get your filthy hands off that coffin," he shouted.

"That right, Henry," said Smith. "Clean your hands first."

"I got nothing to clean them in but the loonshit."

"Take off your shirt and use it for mitts," said Larsen.

Henry and others removed their shirts, used them for mitts and the coffin was transferred, more or less unmuddied, to a nearby knoll.

Many theories of leverage were exchanged.

A Spanish Windlass was a project debated at length. It was a crude machine, which could be constructed of jack-pine poles and rope and gave leverage such as could shift large buildings or overturn railway trains, but although everybody knew some other man who had used a Spanish Windlass, none among this company, it seemed, had done so.

They jacked up the truck and packed in twigs, they jacked it up again and applied larger logs and finally, chewing away jack pines with the dull axe, they built a corduroy road beneath it. On each occasion, Larsen insisted that Smith was not spirited in his use of the gas and each time Smith warned, mildly, that the oil in that ancient engine was low and that the faint tick of the loose bearing was plain to his ear.

It culminated in the corduroy road stage of the operation when Larsen, enraged, shouted, "Smith, pour the coal to her. She'll move. Give her gas."

Smith spoke though the open window, gently. "The bearings are gonna go."

"Shut up and put your foot on the floor."

Smith put his foot on the floor. The tick became a pound. The main bearing seized. A piston went, driving out through the engine block. In the quiet hiss of the steam from a dead engine six men put Ol Antoine's wooden overcoat on their muddy shoulders and began packing it down to the funeral at the Stampede Grounds.

"I will call time for you," said Smith. "It helps. Hup. One. Two. Three. Hup. One. Two. Three.

"He was just a little stick of a man. How can he be so heavy?" said Morton.

"Its Philippine mahogany heartwood, that's why it's heavy," said Smith. "Come on you guys, pick it up," he chanted. "LEFT. LEFT. My father got drunk and he LEFT. LEFT. LEFT."

Half way to their destination, two men from the Reserve met them with a half Percheron pack horse. They roped the coffin on a Visalia pack saddle, but nearing the Stampede Grounds, where the ranchers' camps were at one side, the Indian graveyard at the other, they smelt the smoke of barbecue fires and they could sense the anticipation of the people. Somehow it didn't seem right to bring the old man in on a pack horse, so they unlashed the coffin and brought it out of the trees on their shoulders again. They were caked in mud and so weary they staggered, but they, and those who waited for them, knew the glory.

There was time in the day to spare for the burying so, for the time, all rested, content with accomplishments, gratified to find among the growing crowd faces from far places, faces they had not seen for months or years. What rain was to grass, a funeral was to the society of the Chilcotin plateau.

Smith circled the crowd on the Stampede Grounds, exchanging the occasional greeting, abstractedly accepting congratulations on his splendid ride and his taste in the matter of selecting coffins. His thoughts, it was clear, were in some other place.

He found Norah, busiest of all the women, setting up tables in the community hall.

"I thought I'd go over to our camp and clean up," he said.

"Go ahead, she said, "but seems to me you are the only clean one in the bunch. Why ain't you covered in loonshit like the others?"

"I was a driver. A driver is not a swamper. Why don't you come over with me?"

"Come over why? I gotta set up tables."

"Come on. There's lots of people to set up tables."

"What for?"

"Just come on."

He did not lead her to their tent but instead they went up the sidehill which rose at the edge of the grounds.

"Sit down," he said.

She sat.

"I brought us a mickey. Have a pull."

"You know I can't drink that stuff without water."

"Have a pull, I said."

She put the bottle to pursed lips and blew a bubble into it. He took it and drank richly.

"What are you up to Smith?"

"I am having a drink. With my wife."

"There is something funny about this."

He pushed the bottle toward her. She pushed it back.

"There is something funny about you, Smith."

He gestured to the crowd below them with the little bottle. "Ain't that a pretty sight, Norah? You know, whatever is good about people in Chilacootin, a funeral will bring it out."

It was a pretty sight. Blue smoke rose from the salmon barbecue fires. Small Indian children, doubled up on bareback horses, rode proudly over the stampede grounds. Pickup truck engines muttered politely and in the cabs old friends passed bottles clad in the original brown paper wrappings. Somewhere a guitar played the melody of "Red River Valley," a string at a time. The sun, now turned on to full, shone on Ol Antoine's coffin which stood on a trestle table, guarded by gentle Jim Dan that it might not be smudged by the fingerprints of those who would want to touch it.

"Who is in that coffin, Smith?"

He gave a short sigh. "Rocks," he said.

"Rocks. I see. There is rocks in it."

"I know, you are gonna chew out my ass and bark at the hole. Go ahead."

To spite him, she didn't utter a word.

So he walked her around the subject some more, hoping to take some of the kink out of her backbone.

"You know how it is, Norah. Moccasin telegraph is never right. Ol Antoine just had something done for his eyes at the Lake. When I got back from Prince there he was, cheerful as a sparrow with a mouthful of horseshit, waiting for a ride home."

"I see."

"So I come in by Old Road and they went up to Young Alexander's place and pretty soon they'll come down here. I said they wouldn't want to miss the party and they're comin' down soon."

"That was thoughtful of you Smith, to invite them."

"Of course, s'pose I'd had a gun, I could have shot Ol Antoine when I found him. That way everything could have gone according to plan. Is that what I should have done? Stuck to the plan?"

"You crazy little turd. Can't you see what you have done? You have smashed Larsen's truck . . ."

"He smashed it last month. I did it this month. We are just even."

"You have brought Father Fitzjames riding all night over the mountain . . ."

"There is plenty of baptisms and marriages for him here. His time ain't wasted."

"Shut up. The big thing you have done, your real big accomplishment Smith, you have broke the Namko Cattlemen's Association. Broke them flat, flat, flat."

He waved a hand toward the crowd. "It just didn't seem right to disappoint all them people."

"You could have returned the coffin and got our money back!"

"No, Norah. That is one thing I could not do. It would take too long to explain. Just take my word for it. Nobody in this country would ever have forgiven me if I asked for our money back on that coffin."

She called him a double yoked asshole but, from the way she said it, he could sense that she was just about bucked out for the day.

"Norah," he said. "You and me, we will just sit here a while on this sidehill and watch while Ol Antoine comes down for his funeral. I tell you straight this has the makings of a large and fine day."

She called him a turd again, but this time she was laughing. She took the mickey from his hand and, for the first time, took a good pull of whisky straight.

Champs at the Chuckabug

by
S. OMAR BARKER

"Oh, the Mighty Macs is ropin' men,
With bristles on their chist!
An armless man could use his hands
To count the steers they've missed!"

THAT'S SHORTY McNAC, folks, the rhymin' runt, my poetetic peewee pardner of the rodeos, up on the announcer's stand, makin' say while the Hun shines. Nobody invited him to. These spells jest come on him, same as some dogs got to bark at the moon—even on a cloudy night. Maybe that's the kind of whilly-galoo to make the broncs cheer, but the ache it gives me ain't in my cheerin' muscles.

The point is that right this minute, out yonder in the arid arena of the Chuckabug Champeenship Cowboy Contests, otherwise referred at as a rodeo, a hairy-handed buckaroo named F. X. Hunsaker—Hun fer short—is makin' a money-time tie in the team steer ropin' that'll be as hard to beat as a five-ace hand with a hawgleg behind it. The next steer is up for me an' Shorty, an' yonder he stands, preenin' hisself before the announcer's mike, makin' up rollickin' rhymes fer little folks.

"Shorty!" I squalls at him. "Come down offa that windmill an' grab your whale line! We're up!"

"Jest a minute, Freeholy," he hollers back. "Wait till I say howdy to Granpaw." He grabs the mike ag'in. "Callin' Granpaw McManigan," he bellers. "Granpaw McManigan in the grandstand? Howdy, Granpaw. Say Granpaw, grab a good holt on yer whiskers! The next e-vent is me an' ol' Freeholy ropin' a steer. Your li'l ol' grandson's goin' to show you some cowboyin', the like of which you never seen on the old Chisholm Trail, Granpaw! Watch the arener! The Goshamighty Macs a-comin' out!"

Over in the grandstand I make out a venerable ol' gent rise up off the whiskers he's usin' fer a cushion, raise a long bony ol' arm an' shake his fist at the loud speaker. I cain't make out what he says, but somethin' tells me it ain't got sugar on it.

The ol' gent, you see, is none other than ol' Panhandle McManigan. He ain't Shorty's grandfather, he's mine—an' how he hates it! He's a dynamitish ol' ranny well up in the eighties. He begun throwin' his brand on longhorns an' shovin' 'em up the trails right outa the Ark. He's an ol' time cowman from who skinned the skunk, an' he loves these moderun cowboy sports knowed as rodeo contests the same way he loves ticks in his beard. Cowboys, he claims, the Lord aimed 'em to work cattle on ranch an' range, not go cavortin' around showin' off in front of a grandstand full of dudes an' squatters. Furthermore, he opines, there jest ain't no salt in the cowhands nowdays, anyhow—neither at ridin', ropin' nor nothin' else, compared to the boys he used to ride with.

The fact is, this here is the first rodeo he's ever come to watch, an' that's one reason it's up to me an' my runt pardner to git out there an' tie steers to beat all hell with the hide on. I've had to plumb hogtie him to drag him here in the first place. But me an' Shorty have made him a bet: if we don't convince him that we're the ropin'est, steer-tyin'est team his agin' eyes ever lit on, we've agreed to quit rodeoin' an' go to cow nursin' on his ranch. While if our performance is good enough to make him acknowledge the corn, he's goin' to finance us across the Big C Water to compete in Tex Austin's world champeenship contests in London. An' that ain't all. Me, Freeholy McManigan, main buckarooster of the Goshamighty Macs rodeo pardnership, I'm his only livin' heir—an' Granpaw McManigan is a man that carries enough green-backs around in his pockets to choke a steer. But he ain't too old to write me out of his will if he takes the notion.

An' with that the lay, Shorty McNac has to stand up there on the windmill wisecrackin', when our turn's done been called for the steer ropin'. Not only that, he's got to take a razz at Granpaw's whiskers, about which Granpaw is as touchy as a raw bronc about his heel feathers.

"Hey, you, Freeholy!" hollers the Arena Director. "Your steer's a-waitin'. Git on out here!"

At long last Shorty has started wedgin' his way outa the gang that always packs the announcer's little bird house, but some drug store cowboy in a pink shirt, a stranger in these parts, throws an arm plumb familiar around Shorty's shoulder the way a lot of these hangers-on is always doin' us champs, an' delays him.

The results is that when the Goshamighty Macs finally leaves the startin' chute after a big ol' spotted steer, we've done got a ten-second fine hung onto us by the judges for bein' late on the line. Behind us I can hear this here Hun Hunsaker's time bein' announced. It's twenty-three seconds, flat—which is plenty fast to tie a steer in any rodeo.

To match it, we'd have to make ours in thirteen. Same chance as a feller's got of spittin' over the moon.

This team steer ropin', one man ropes the head. Soon as he ketches, the other 'un rushes in an' jerks a loop onto the ranny's heels, thus stretchin' him flat frum both ends. It bein' the job of the head-roper, then, to fly outa the saddle with a hoggin' string an' tie the steer down.

"Git 'im, Freeholy!" Shorty hollers at me, as we take out. "Loop them ol' horns fer Granpaw!"

It always helps, when you're mad, to have the feller that got you that way squallin' at you. Yeah, I miss the first loop. My second drops purty, Shorty picks up his heels, an' I step off to tie. Like as not we're still makin' third money time. But whilst I don't make no practice of listenin' to the grandstand, this time I hear Granpaw McManigan's ol' bobbed-wire voice squallin' at me, plumb full of ol' Chisholm Trail razzberries to the effect that he'll send me out supper an' a bed-roll if I'm aimin' to take all night. If I hadn't been harkin' to him I wouldn't never have let that ol' steer's tail swish me in the eyes like it done, an' it full of cockleburrs.

"The Goshamighty Macs' time," booms the loud speaker as we finally ride back to the chutes, "fifty-one seconds, includin' the penalty!"

From the grandstand, suspiciously close to where ol' Granpaw's whiskers looms up like a white hoss-tail at midnight, comes a noise like somebody rippin' wet overalls. It's nice to have your own kinfolks cheerin' you thataway.

Huns Hunsaker an' High-Nose Mugler, his ropin' pardner, holds their noses an' grins at us as we come a-past 'em to the bleachers. An' dinged if this here pink-shirt drugstore cowboy that's hangin' around, actin' the pal with ary cowboy that lets him—dinged if he don't put in his word:

"Nice week's work, boys," he says.

The only reason I didn't hit him in the nose is that he dodges too quick, an' Hunsaker steps between us. I'd of hit him, too, but Shorty grabs me by the shirt tail.

"Remember Granpaw," he says, "an' don't git yourself crippled!"

Trouble with Shorty, he don't never take nothin' serious. He climbs up on the windmill ag'in, edges in a-past the announcer an' commences broadcastin' once more, somethin' like this:

"Oh, Granpaw do not wave yore beard,
It skeers both broncs an' men!
Yore boys ain't—"

That's as far as he gits. Right there this announcer feller jumps straight up in the air an' comes down snortin'. He's reached in his pocket for money to pay a bet, an' the said pocket pulls a Mother Hubbard's cubbard on him.

"Yow!" he hollers. "I been robbed!"

He begins runnin' his hands through his other pockets an' lets out yowl No. 2. His watch is gone, also.

Well, to make this chapter short but not sweet, the Deputy Sheriff on duty, ol' Bill Gordon, he searches ever'body up there in the stand right pronto. He don't find no money, but he does find this announcer's valuable gold watch—in Shorty McNac's pants pockit.

Come the dawn of the second day of the Chuckabug Rodeo, an' Shorty McNac takes breakfast in the hoosegow. I been on circle all night tryin' to find somebody to put up the money to bail him out, but ever' waddy I hit claims he's just spent his last nickel for a sandwich, an' why don't I git my Granpaw to bail him out? Ol' Panhandle's got plenty money, ain't he? But they don't know Granpaw.

Finally, 'bout eight A.M. I wrastle my nerves together an' interview Granpaw. I don't beat around the gooseberry bush none, either.

"Granpaw," I says, "loan me the money to bail Shorty outa jail."

"What's the matter?" he crackles through his beard. "Ain't it a good jail?"

"Fair," I says. "But Granpaw, I cain't win no steer ropin' contest without my pardner."

"No," he says, "nor with him. How much you want?"

I tell him two hunderd, an' of course he'll git it back, as Shorty won't duck the trial.

"Tell you what," he allows, "I'll offer twice that to put you in with him."

"Skeered of losin' yer bet, Granpaw?" I taunts him.

"No," he says, "I'm skeered I'll win it—an' have a coupla useless rodeodoers on my hands. Come on, let's go see if that jassack pardner of yours has growed hair on his ears yet."

After seein' the judge an' makin' bail, we proceeds to the jail and find that Shorty hasn't, but one look at him tells me he's sproutin' with poetry—which is worse.

"Aha, Granpaw," he warbles, "I jest been makin' up a pome for you! Listen:

"Oh, Granpaw, he's an' ol' he wolf,
Few old 'uns is much brisker.
But he cain't eat soup nor swing a loop,
'Cause he runs too strong to whisker!"

"Yah-gh-gh!" growls Granpaw an' starts to swing on him.

"Wup, here!" says the jailer. "You cain't hit a prizner!"

"Then unprizner him!" yowls Granpaw. "I've paid cash fer his bail! Here's your papers. Turn 'im out, the under-growed, tickbearin' son of a circus monkey, an' let me at him!"

So the jailer turns ol' Shorty out. I reckon if Granpaw hadn't tripped on his beard, he'd of ketched him the first fifty yards, but as it happens, Shorty out-scoots him.

By afternoon I've got Granpaw cooled off to where he comes to the rodeo agin. I've warned Shorty to stay clear of him, but when the announcer won't let him up to the mike to orate, no doubt fearful of losin' his watch ag'in, the runt buzzes over to the grandstand, claimin' he's goin' to make up an' be pals with Granpaw.

"Trouble with you," he complains to me, "you take Granpaw too serious. These ol' rannyhans, you got to jolly 'em along."

Well, it's while this Hun Hunsaker-High Nose Mugler steer team is ropin' that the rumpus busts out in the grandstand. Shorty had crowded in alongside of Granpaw, the ol' ranny has biffed him in the nose, Shorty to keep from fallin' on a lady with twins, has grabbed aholt of Granpaw's whiskers, an' at this point a feller in a pink shirt, settin' next to Granpaw on the other side, has butted in, an' a dog-fight-time is had by all—for about two seconds, till the Chuckabug Firemen, actin' as ushers, grabs Shorty an' hustles him out.

It's a good thing, too, because the next minute the Mighty Macs is called for the steer ropin'. We miss a late start by a gnat's wink, but we make up for it like a wolf over-haulin' a badger. I'm head-ropin' an' tyin' ag'in today, account of Shorty bein' too worked up an' winded from his row in the grandstand; and we shore make sweet time on it: twenty-one and one-fifth seconds, believe it or take pizen.

That puts our total on two steers up to seventy-two and one-fifth seconds. Only one team has us topped: Hun Hunsaker with sixty-nine seconds on two steers. This is a three steer contest an' in spite of our bad bust the first day, we still got a chance to win it. All we got to do is beat the time of ol' Hun an' High-Nose tomorrow by three an' two-fifth seconds, an' the champ purse is ours.

But more important even than that, we're showin' ol' Granpaw what a coupla moderun rodeo steer ropers can do when their whale lines is really hot. Ol' Granpaw may have his faults but an old cowhand like him knows honest-to-thunder-grease steer ropin' when he sees it.

"I reckon that tie will convince him," I observes to Shorty as we start back to the chutes.

"Yeah?" grunts Shorty. "Been me on the *tie,* we'd of made it twenty seconds flat. What was you doin', puttin' a necktie bow on him? Wait till tomorrow, I'll show you how to tie a steer without takin' all week to it. Hey, looky yonder! What's goin' on?"

It's a rumpus in the grandstand ag'in, and dinged if Granpaw ain't right in the middle of it, wavin' his whiskers, high, wild an' handsome. He's all worked up over somethin', an' it ain't our fast ropin' nor a bee loose in his britches, neither. In fact he ain't even *seen* that quick tie of mine. In plain words, without no hem-hawin', he's been robbed. He's had his pocket picked of a roll containin' right around one thousand dollars. He's just now discovered it, but he thinks Shorty McNac done it before he got hustled out of the grandstand. It looks like the Goshamighty Mac has been run into a bog an' got tamped down.

Robbery or no robbery, the show out in the arena has got to go right on. There's some two thousand folks in the grandstand that has paid cash money to see a rodeo, an' the Chuckabug management ain't goin' to let 'em down. The show goes on. But not for Granpaw McManigan.

Him an' Deputy Sheriff Bill Gordon, the Fire Chief that's head usher, me an' Shorty McNac an' several others holds a council of war back under the grandstand.

"Looky here, Granpaw," I says, might' nigh havin' to knot his whiskers around my wrist to hold his attention. "I been pardnerin' with Shorty McNac for five years, rain or shine. He's a runt, he's a poetizin' punk, he's a grandstandin' gazimpus, he puts cactus on the chairs at the rodeo dances, he eats soup with a pocketknife, he climbs on broncs backwards if you don't watch him, his feet sweats plumb ruinous, he makes kissin' noises in his sleep, an' whistles through his ears, but he ain't no thief! An' if he was, he's too but-terfingered to pick the pockets of a dead man without bringin' him to life. You're barkin' up the wrong tree, Granpaw!"

"Ain't no tree," says Granpaw, "an' I ain't barkin' up it nohow. I been robbed, young feller. What you figger me to do, lay down an' wag my tail about it?"

"You sure that money ain't lost somewheres in that spinach?" says Shorty. "I knowed a feller lost a curry comb in his whiskers once, an'—"

"I've knowed fellers to lose their wind, too," growls Granpaw, "on the end of a rope."

He glares at Shorty, plumb significant.

"Granpaw," I says, "I'm a McManigan, the same as you. Shorty McNac is my pardner, an' I'll vouch for him!"

"Vouch an' be damned," says Granpaw. "Who's goin' to vouch fer my money?"

"I will," says Shorty McNac all of a sudden, drawin' himself up. "You've lost your cash, now that's a fack. Well, the Mighty Macs will git it back. We brung you here, an' by dad-gum-it, we aim to see you don't lose frum it! If your money ain't found by tomorrow night, we'll use our winnin's to make it right. We'll win five hundred in the team steer-tyin'. First money, I tell you, without half tryin'! An' the rest," he goes on, runnin' outa rhymes, "we'll pay out, ridin' for you on your ranch!"

"God forbid!" says Granpaw.

But finally he listens to reason. He searches Shorty an' don't find nothin'. Then he's all fer searchin' ever' man, woman an' child in the grandstand, ever' contestant, arena hand, clown, bronc and mule ear in the whole durn rodeo park, but at the suggestion of this here pink-shirted stranger who is attendin' the conference, he finally agrees it ain't no use to search contestants that was out in the arena when it happened. An' ol' Bill Gordon stands fast for the idee that they'll only search everybody seated anywheres near Granpaw in the grandstand, an' all the ushers an' popcorn peddlers that's been passin' by him off and on.

But of course the search, beginnin' on this pink-shirted stranger his ownself, an' even includin' the lady with twins, nets jest exactly nothin' with a hole in it.

"Shorty McNac," I says, that evenin' at our camp, after we've licked the beanpot clean, an' mighty little prospect of ever seein' it full ag'in, "do you realize that the Goshamighty Macs is marooned on a sinkin' island plumb out in the middle of the crick, with the quicksands of trouble an' tribulation extendin' forty miles in all directions?"

Shorty lays off the mouth harp long enough to grin.

"Ain't we been bogged down before," he chides me, "an' come out ringin' our tails? You jest leave it to Shorty, ol' hoss."

"Damned if I ain't a-notion to!"

Then I kinder tally it up for him. We've come to the Chuckabug Contests busted, but otherwise as carefree an' sprouty as a coupla friskin' colts in a clover field. An' look at our saddle sores now! Tied up on a bet with ol' Granpaw that we're plumb sure to lose; all our winnin's, if we do get in the first money, done pledged an' promised to Granpaw to make up for him lettin' some smoothie run a hand into his pockets; Shorty under bail to stand up before a jury an' prove somebody else put that announcer's watch in his pocket: an' for me, ol' Granpaw McManigan snortin' to high heaven that he'll disown, disinherit an' probly plumb disjoint me for ever sayin' "rodeo" to him in the first place. Not to mention the prospect of havin' to quit contestin' an' go to tackin' up fences on Granpaw's ranch at about eight dollars a month till he figgers he's paid up.

"Shorty," I winds up, "come dark, let's pack up an' drift, while the driftin's good."

Shorty finishes up the tune he's playin', as unconcerned as a gooful bird with a crop full of minnie bugs.

"The wolf that spooks an' runs away," he orates, "gits trapped an' skun some other day!"

"Yeah," I says, "an' for them that don't, as the Mighty Macs is due to learn to their sorrow, that fatal day ain't no further off than about four P.M. tomorrow."

"Your poetry," says Shorty, "is lousy."

Maybe it is, but it don't get me arrested for swipin' watches.

The third day of the Chuckabug Rodeo opens with a bango, an' to my surprise, ol' Granpaw is settin' out on the chute-bleachers amongst the hands.

"Welcome, Granpaw," I greets him, with a smile full of good will an' back teeth. "Today you're goin' to see some shore 'nough steer tyin'."

"Yeah?" he snorts. "How about tyin' the bull, first?"

Ol' Hun Hunsaker, High-Nose Mugler an' this smart aleck drugstore cowboy in the pink shirt all happen to be within hearin' an' they join Granpaw in givin' me the horse laugh.

"Gonna bust the record today, are yuh?" says ol' Hun. "Which one of you's gonna tie?"

"I am," Shorty busts in, "an'—"

"Got any talkin' money?" says ol' Hun. "I got a fifty here that says you don't tie under forty seconds. Do I hear an' answer?"

Not from me he don't. Not with only a mortgaged thirty cents in my pocket. But Shorty McNac takes him up like a whip:

"Double it that we tie in thirty!" he snaps.

"O' course you got the money?" sneers ol' Hun.

"I got my saddle," says Shorty, "that's worth one fifty."

It's silver-mounted prize saddle that Hun Hunsaker had craved mighty bad to win at Las Vegas, but that Shorty had out rode him for. Now it looks like Hun's goin' to have it after all. It's a damn fool bet, but Shorty won't listen to reason.

Out yonder the Arena Director has begun callin' out the ropin' order, an' we got to git to our places, as we're second up. I notice this pink-shirt guy walks out with Shorty to his horse.

"You're a dead game sport, cowboy," he says. "I'm for you."

So he is, is he? The way Shorty McNac lopes up on the big steer when they turn him out, he'd better be! It's a fast ketch an' a sure one. I jerk a loop on his heels, an' we stretch that rannyhan so neat an' quick that it even brings ol' Granpaw up out of his beard.

"Whoopy-yee!" he yowls. "Now let's see what kind of a cowhand ye be, little squirt!"

The way things stands, a mighty lot depends on Shorty tyin' that steer in record time, an' the way he flies off an' takes to him, it

makes me think fer a second that my peewee pardner is shore goin'
to yank us Mighty Macs out of the boghole.

"Wrap 'im up, Shorty!" I hollers, to encourage him. "He's yore
packidge!"

But instid of grapplin' the ol' steer's legs an' makin' the tie,
pronto, Shorty jest stands over him lookin' kinder dazed. Then he
lets out a squall like the wail of a cattymount with a knot in his
tail—an' I see what ails him: he's reached for the hoggin' string, otherwise knowed as the tyin' rope, in his belt—an' it ain't there! An'
me, not bein' due to tie, I ain't carryin' one, neither.

You cain't hogtie a steer with your imagination. It's a bitter
moment for the Mighty Macs. What I hear ol' Granpaw yellin' from
the bleachers don't sweeten it none, either.

"Use poetry on 'im, cowboy!" he's yellin'. "Use poetry!"

Well, it looks like the Chuckabug contest is done over, as far as
the Mighty Macs is concerned. I'm jest startin' to slack up to turn the
ol' steer a-loose, when I see Shorty McNac jerkin' off his pants! In
about half a gnat's wink, believe it or take pizen, Shorty McNac has
got three of that steer's legs hogtied with 'em, an' bein' Levi's, they
hold. Shorty, in shirt tail an' underbritches, throws up his hand to signal "tied," the time flag drops—and the grandstand goes plumb wild.

"The Goshamighty Macs' time," bellers the announcer, "thirty seconds flat. That's a world's record, folks for puttin' pants on a steer!"

Maybe it is, but it would of been under twenty if Shorty had
had his string, an' thirty seconds ain't li'ble to win us no contest,
not with the lead ol' Hunsaker has already got. He can take thirty-
three seconds to tie his third steer an' still beat us.

But who cares a tinker's damn about that now? For when we
come back to the bleachers, takin' our bow, there's ol' Granpaw
doin' an Injun war dance an' flaggin' us with his whiskers.

"That there's cowboyin'!" he yells, plumb delighted. "That's ol'
time cowboyin', you sons of the curly wolf, like we done on the ol'
Chisholm Trail! I seen that feller swipe your hoggin' string, Shorty,

but I never said nothin'! Jest wanted to see, by cracky, if you was cowboy enough to meet an emergency. Yessir, an'—"

"Seen *who* swipe my hawgin' string?" hollers Shorty.

"Why, that there what's-his-name in the pink shirt, when he went pal-in' you out to your hoss! He—"

For once Shorty McNac don't pause for poetry. He don't tarry, in fact for nothin', except to spot that pink shirt somewheres over in the grandstand—not even to put on his pants. He jumps the track fence like a bowlegged jackrabbit an' goes tearin' up into the grandstand, knockin' folks right an' left. He grabs that pink-shirt guy like a wolf grabs a yearlin', an' comes draggin' him out to the chutes. From yonder at the hot dog stand ol' Deputy Sheriff Bill Gordon comes a-pantin' an' a-puffin' to see what's up.

It's plenty.

"Here, Granpaw," says Shorty, shovin' the pink shirt plumb into Granpaw's whiskers. "Here's yer ol' pickpocket!"

"But," says Bill Gordon, buttin' in, "you ain't got no evidence!"

"Maybe not," grins Shorty McNac, "but there ain't *nobody* but a perfessional pickpocket lightfingered enough to swipe my hoggin' string off me, or plant a stole watch on me. If he done that, he also—"

All of a sudden this Pink-Shirt starts to jerk away. It's contact with the ham on the end of my right arm that stops him.

I hear the Arena Director bellerin' up the ropers. He's callin' Hun Hunsaker an' High-Nose Mugler. But Shorty McNac steps into that dogfight, too, mighty sudden.

"Git High-Nose, Freeholy!" he says. "I'll git ol' Hun!"

Without askin' him why nor how come, I swing my loop. For a minute it's a dogfight, with these two buckos fightin' our lass ropes that's settled so sudden down onto 'em. It plumb stops the show.

But not for long. The deputy searches 'em. Sewed away inside their shirts they've got most o' Granpaw's swiped money, an' some more, to boot.

I wouldn't never have figgered it out, but ol' Shorty had.

"Ever' time a pocket was picked," he explains, "it was while ol' Hun an' High-Nose was out in the arena—so they wouldn't be suspected. An' quick as they come in, ol' Pink-Shirt slipped 'em the money, that's all."

Well, ol' Hun an' High-Nose, bein' proved crooked, the judges plumb elaminoote them from the contest—which leaves the Mighty Macs drawin' first money in the team steer ropin'. But it ain't enough to finance us to that big rodeo of Tex's comin' off in London, acrost the Big C Water. An' ol' Granpaw don't seem to be plumb convinced that us moderun punchers measures up to the ol' time standard—even yet.

"Boys," he says, curryin' his beard mighty solemn. "Accordin' to the agreement, you got to come out to work on my ranch, ain't you? You be ready tomorrow at—"

"Damn your whiskers, Granpaw!" I explode. "We ketched your thief! We—"

"Don't interrupt me thataway," says Granpaw sternly, wroppin' his beard thoughtfully about his left ear. "Two weeks on the ranch I'll give you to convince me you're worth your salt as cowhands. If you don't make good, jinged if I don't aim to ship you off plumb to London or some place—at my own expense!"

Up behind the spinach ol' Granpaw's eyes kinder twinkles. The three of us swaps grins. Then Shortly McNac, waxin' poetic again, though still pantsless, r'ars back on his haunches:

"Oh, the Mighty Macs is ropin' men,
From who-so laid the chunk—
An' for a fack, ol' Granpaw Mac,
He's smarter than we thunk!"

Rain on the Range

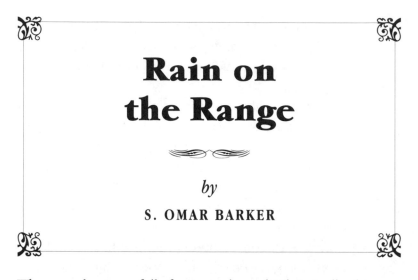

by

S. OMAR BARKER

When your boots are full of water and your hat brim's all a-drip,
And the rain makes little rivers dribblin' down your horse's hip,
When every step your pony takes, it purt near bogs him down,
It's then you git to thinkin' of them boys that work in town.
They're maybe sellin' ribbon, or they're maybe slingin' hash,
But they've got a roof above 'em when the thunder starts to crash.
They do their little doin's, be their wages low or high,
But let it rain till hell's a pond, they're always warm and dry.
Their beds are stuffed with feathers, or at worst with plenty straw,
While your ol' soggy soogans* may go floatin' down the draw.
They've got no rope to fret about that kinks up when it's wet;
There ain't no puddle formin' in the saddle where they set.
There's womenfolks to cook 'em up the chuck they most admire
While you gnaw cold, hard biscuits 'cause the cook can't build a fire.

When you're ridin' on the cattle range and hit a rainy spell,
Your whiskers git plumb mossy, and you note a mildewed smell
On everything from leather to the makin's in your sack;
And you git the chilly quivers from the water down your back.
You couldn't pull your boots off if you hitched 'em to a mule;

You think about them ribbon clerks, and call yourself a fool
For ever punchin' cattle with a horse between your knees,
Instead of sellin' ribbons and a-takin' of your ease.
You sure do git to ponderin' about them jobs in town,
Where slickers ain't a drippin' when the rain comes sluicin' down.
It's misery in your gizzard, and you sure do aim to quit,
And take most any sheltered job you figger you can git.
But when you've got your neck all bowed to quit without a doubt,
The rain just beats you to it, and the sun comes bustin' out!
Your wet clothes start to steamin', and most everywhere you pass
You notice how that week of rain has livened up the grass.
That's how it is with cowboys when a rainy spell is hit:
They hang on till it's over—then there ain't no need to quit!

*soogans or sougan, a quilt or comforter in a cowboy's bedrole

Science at Heart's Desire

by

EMERSON HOUGH

"THAT OLD RAILROAD'LL SHORE BUST ME UP a heap if it ever does git in here," remarked Tom Osby one morning in the forum of Whiteman's corral, where the accustomed group was sitting in the sun, waiting for some one to volunteer as Homer for the day.

There was little to do but listen to story telling, for Tom Osby dwelt in the tents of Kedar, delaying departure on his accustomed trip to Vegas.

"A feller down there to Sky Top," he went on, arousing only the most indolent interest, "one of them spy-glass ingineers—tenderfoot, with his six-shooter belt buckled so tight he couldn't get his feet to the ground—he says to me I might as well trade my old grays for a nice new checkerboard, or a deck of author cards, for I won't have nothing to do but just amuse myself when the railroad cars gets here."

No one spoke. All present were trying to imagine how Heart's Desire would seem with a railroad train each day.

"Things'll be some different in them days, mebbe so." Tom recrossed his legs with well-considered deliberation.

"There's a heap of things different already from what they used to be when I first hit the cow range," said Curly. "The whole country's changed, and it ain't changed for the better, either. Grass is longer, and horns is shorter, and men is triflin'er. Since the Yankees has got west of the Missouri River, a ranch foreman ain't allowed to run his own brandin' iron any more, and that takes morc'n half the poetry out of the cow business, don't it, Mac?" This to McKinney, who was nearly asleep.

"Everything else is changin', too," Curly continued, gathering fluency as memories began to crowd upon him. "Look at the lawyers and doctors there is in the Territory now—and this country used to be respectable. Why, when I first come here, there wasn't a doctor within a thousand miles, and no need for one. If one of the boys got shot up much, we always found some way to laundry him and sew him together again without no need of a diplomy. No one ever got sick; and, of course, no one ever did die of his own accord, the way they do back in the States."

"What's it all about, Curly?" drawled Dan Anderson. "You can't tell a story worth a cent." Curly paid no attention to him.

"The first doctor that ever come out here for to alleviate us fellers," he went on, "why, he settled over on the Sweetwater. He was a allopath from Bitter Creek. What medicine that feller did give! He gradual drifted into the vet'inary line.

"Then there come a homeopath—that was after a good many women-folk had settled in along the railroad over west. Still, there wasn't much sickness, and I don't reckon the homeopath ever did winter through. I was livin' with the Bar-T outfit on the Oscura range, at that time.

"Next doctor that come along was a ostypath." Curly took a chew of tobacco, and paused a moment reflectively.

"I said the first feller drifted into vet'inary lines, didn't I?" he resumed. "Well, the ostypath did, too. Didn't you never hear about that? Why, he ostypathed a horse!"

"Did *what?*" asked Tom Osby, sitting up; for hitherto there had seemed no need to listen attentively.

"Yes, sir," he went on, "he ostypathed a horse for us. The boys they gambled about two thousand dollars on that horse over at Socorro. It was a cross-eyed horse, too."

"What's that?" Doc Tomlinson objected. "There never was such a thing as a cross-eyed horse."

"Oh, there wasn't, wasn't there?" said Curly, "Well, now, my friend, when you talk that-a-way, you simply show me how much you don't know about horses. This here Bar-T horse was as cross-eyed as a sawhorse, until we got him ostypathed. But, of course, if you don't believe what I say, there's no use tellin' you this story at all."

"Oh, go on, go on," McKinney spoke up, "don't pay no attention to doc."

"Well," Curly resumed, "that there horse was knowed constant on this range for over three years. He was a outlaw, with cream mane and tail, and a *pinto* map of Europe, Asia and Africa wrote all over his ribs. Run? Why, that horse could run down a coyote as a moral pastime. We used him to catch jackrabbits with, between meals. It wasn't no trouble for him to *run*. The trouble was to tell when he was goin' to *stop* runnin'. Sometimes it was a good while before the feller ridin' him could get him around to where he begun to run. He run in curves natural, and he handed out a right curve or a left one, just as he happened to feel, same as the feller dealin' faro, and just as easy.

"Tom Redmond, on the Bar T, he got this horse from a feller by the name of Hasenberg, that brought in a bunch of a has-beens and outlaws, and allowed to distribute 'em in this country. Hasenberg was a foreign gent that looked a good deal like Whiteman, our distinguished feller citizen here. He was cross-eyed hisself, body and soul. There wasn't a straight thing about him. We allowed that maybe this pinto *caballo* got cross-eyed from associatin' with old Hasenberg, who was strictly on the bias, any way you figured."

"You ain't so bad, after all, Curly," said Dan Anderson, sitting up. "You're beginning now to hit the human interest part. You ought to be a reg'lar contributor."

"Shut up!" said Curly. "Now Tom Redmond, he took to this here pinto horse from havin' seen him jump the corral fence several times, and start floatin' off across the country for a eight or ten mile sashay without no special encouragement. He hired three Castilian busters to operate on pinto, and he got so he could be rode occasional, but every one allowed they never did see any horse just like him. He was the most aggravatinest thing we ever did have on this range. He had a sort of odd-lookin' white eye, but a heap of them pintos has got glass eyes, and so no one thought to examine his lookers very close, though it was noticed early in the game that pinto might be lookin' one way and goin' the other, at the same time. He'd be goin' on a keen lope, and then something or other might get on his mind, and he'd stop and untangle hisself from all kinds of ridin'. Sometimes he'd jump and snort like he was seein' ghosts. A feller on that horse could have roped antelopes as easy as yearlin' calves, if he could just have told which way Mr. Pinto was goin'; but he was a shore hard one to estermate.

"At last Tom, why, he suspected somethin' wasn't right with pinto's lamps. If you stuck out a bunch of hay at him, he couldn't bite it by about five feet. When you led him down to water, you had to go sideways; and if you wanted to get him in through the corral gate, you had to push him in backward. We discovered right soon that he was born with his parallax or something out of gear. His graduated scale of seein' things was different from our'n. I don't reckon anybody ever will know what all pinto saw with them glass lamps of his, but all the time we knowed that if we could ever onct get his lookin' outfit turned up proper, we had the whole country skinned in a horse race; for he could shore run copious.

"That was why he had the whole Bar-T outfit guessin' all the time. We all wanted to bet on him, and we was all scared to. Sometimes we'd make up a purse among us, and we'd go over to some social gatherin' or other and win a thousand dollars. Old pinto could run all day; he can yet, for that matter. Didn't make no difference to him how often we raced him; and natural, after we'd won one hatful of money with him, we'd want to win another. That was where our judgment was weak.

"You never could tell whether pinto was goin' to finish under the wire, or out in the landscape. His eyes seemed to be sort of moverable, but like enough they'd get sot when he went to runnin'. Then he'd run whichever way he was lookin' at the time, or happened to think he was lookin'; and dependin' additional on what he thought he saw. And law! A whole board of supervisors and school commissioners couldn't have looked that horse in the face, and guessed on their sacred honor whether he was goin' to jump the fence to the left or take to the high sage on the outside of the track.

"Oncet in a while we'd git pinto's left eye set at a angle, and he'd come around the track and under the wire before she wobbled out of place. On them occasions we made money a heap easier than I ever did a-gettin' it from home. But, owin' to the looseness of them eyes, I don't reckon there never was no horse racin' as uncertain as this here; and like enough you may have observed it's uncertain enough even when things is fixed in the most comf'terble way possible."

A deep sigh greeted this, which showed that Curly's audience was in full sympathy.

"You always felt like puttin' the saddle on to pinto hind end to, he was so cross-eyed," he resumed ruminatingly, "but still you couldn't help feelin' sorry for him, neither. Now, he had a right pained and grieved look in his face all the time. I reckon he thought this was a hard sort of a world to get along in. It is. A cross-eyed man has a hard enough time, but a cross-eyed *horse*—well, you don't know how much trouble he can be for hisself and every one else around him.

"Now, here we was, fixed up like I told you. Mr. Allopath is over on Sweetwater creek, Mr. Homeopath is maybe in the last stages of starvation. Old pinto looks plumb hopeless, and all us fellers is mostly hopeless too, owin' to his uncertain habits in a horse race, yet knowin' that it ain't perfessional for us not to back a Bar-T horse that can run as fast as this one can.

"About then along come Mr. Ostypath. This was just about thirty days before the county fair at Socorro, and there was money hung up for horse races over there that made us feel sick to think of. We knew we could go out of the cowpunchin' business for good if we could just only onct get pinto over there, and get him to run the right way for a few brief moments.

"Was he game? I don't know. There never was no horse ever got clost enough to him in a horse race to tell whether he was game or not. He might not get back home in time for supper, but he would shore run industrious. Say, I talked in a telyphome onct. The book hung on the box said the telyphome was instantaneous. It ain't. But now this pinto, he was a heap more instantaneous than a telyphome.

"As I was sayin', it was long about now Mr. Ostypath comes in. He talks with the boss about locatin' around in here. Boss studies him over a while, and as there ain't been anybody sick for over ten years, he tries to break it to Mr. Ostypath gentle that the Bar T ain't a good place for a doctor. They have some conversation along in there, that-a-way, and Mr. Ostypath before long gets the boss interested deep and plenty. He says there ain't no such a thing as gettin' sick. We all knew that before; but he certainly floors the lot when he allows that the reason a feller don't feel good, so as he can eat tenpenny nails, and make a million dollars a year, is always because there is something wrong with his osshus structure.

"He says the only thing that makes a feller have rheumatism, or dyspepsia, or headache, or nosebleed, or red hair, or any other sickness, is that something is wrong with his nervous system. Now, it's this-a-way. He allows them nerves is like a bunch of garden hose. If you put your foot on the hose, the water can't run right free. If you take it off, everything's lovely. 'Now,' says Mr. Ostypath, 'if, owin' to some luxation, some leeshun, some temporary mechanical disarrangement of your osshus structure, due to a oversight of a All-wise Providence, or maybe a fall off'n a buckin' horse, one of them bones of yours gets to pressin' on a nerve, why, it ain't natural you *ought* to feel good. Now, *is* it?' says he.

"He goes on and shows how all up and down a feller's backbone there is plenty of soft spots, and he shows likewise that there is scattered around in different parts of a feller's territory something like two hundred and four and a half bones, any one of which is likely any minute to jar loose and go to pressin' on a soft spot; 'In which case,' says he, 'there is need of a ostypath immediate.'

"'For instance,' he says to me, 'I could make quite a man out of you in a couple of years if I had the chanct.' I ast him what his price would be for that, and he said he was willin' to tackle it for about fifty dollars a month. That bein' just five dollars a month more than the boss was allowin' me at the time, and me seein' I'd have to go about two years without anything to wear or eat—let alone anything to drink—I had to let this chanct go by. I been strugglin' along, as you know, ever since, just like this, some shopworn, but so's to set up. There was one while, I admit when the doc made me some nervous, when I thought of all them soft spots in my spine, and all them bones liable to get loose any minute and go to pressin' on them. But I had to take my chances, like any other cow puncher at forty-five a month."

"You ought to raise his wages, Mac," said Doc Tomlinson to McKinney, the ranch foreman, but the latter only grunted.

"Mr. Ostypath, he stayed around the Bar T quite a while," began Curly again, "and we got to talkin' to him a heap about modern science. Says he, one evenin', this-a-way to us fellers, says he, 'Why, a great many things goes wrong because the nervous system is interfered with, along of your osshus structure. You think your stomach is out of whack,' says he. 'It ain't. All it needs is more nerve supply. I git that by loosenin' up the bones in your back. Why, I've cured a heap of rheumatism, and paralysis, and cross-eyes, and—'

"'What's that?' says Tom Redmond, right sudden.

"'You heard me, sir,' says the doc, severe.

"Tom, he couldn't hardly wait, he was so bad struck with the idea he had. 'Come here, doc,' says he. And then him and doc walked off a little ways and begun to talk. When they come up toward us again, we heard the doc sayin': 'Of course I could cure him. Straybismus is dead easy. I never did operate on no horse, but I've got to eat, and if this here is the only patient in this whole blamed country, why I'll have to go you, if it's only for the sake of science,' says he. Then we all bunched in together and drifted off toward the corral, where old pinto was standin', lookin' hopeless and thoughtful. 'Is this the patient?' says the doc, sort of sighin'.

"'It are,' says Tom Redmond.

"Doc he walks up to old pinto, and has a look at him, front-ways, sideways and all around. Pinto raises his head up, snorts, and looks doc full in the face; leastwise, if he'd 'a' been any other horse, he'd 'a' been lookin' him full in the face. Doc he stands thoughtful for quite a while, and then he goes and kind of runs his hand up and down along pinto's spine. He growed plumb enthusiastic then. 'Beautiful subject,' says he. 'Be-*yoo*-tiful ostypathic subject! Whole osshus structure exposed!' And pinto shore was a dream if bones was needful in the game."

Curly paused for another chew of tobacco, then went on again.

"Well, it's like this, you see; the backbone of a man or a horse is full of little humps—you can see that easy in the springtime. Now old pinto's back, it looked like a topygraphical survey of the whole Rocky Mountain range.

"Doc he runs his hand up and down along this high divide, and says he, 'Just like I thought,' says he. 'The patient has suffered a distinct leeshun in the immediate vicinity of his vaseline motor centers.'"

"You mean the vasomotor centers," suggested Dan Anderson.

"That's what I said," said Curly, aggressively.

"Now, when we all heard doc say them words, we knowed he was shore scientific, and we come up clost while the examination was progressin'.

"'Most extraordinary,' says doc, feelin' some more. 'Now, here is a distant luxation in the lumber regions.' He talked like pinto had a wooden leg.

"'I should diagnose great cerebral excitation, along with pernounced ocular hesitation,' says doc at last.

"'Now look here, doc,' says Tom Redmond to him then. 'You go careful. We all know there's something strange about this here horse; but now, if he's got any bone pressin' on him anywhere that makes him *run* the way he does, why, you be blamed careful not to money with that there particular bone. Don't you touch his *runnin'* bone, because *that's* all right the way it is.'

"'Don't you worry any,' says the doc. 'All I should do would only increase his nerve supply. In time I could remedy his ocular defecks, too,' says he. He allows that if we will give him time, he can make pinto's eyes straighten out so's he'll look like a new rockin' horse Christmas mornin' at a church festerval. Incidentally he suggests that we get a tall leather blinder and run it down pinto's nose, right between his eyes.

"This last was what caught us most of all. 'This here blinder idea,' says Tom Redmond, 'is plumb scientific. The trouble with us cowpunchers is we ain't got no brains—or we wouldn't be cowpunchers! Now look here, pinto's right eye looks off to the left, and his left eye looks off to the right. Like enough he sees all sorts of things on both sides of him, and gets 'em mixed. Now, you put this here harness leather between his eyes, and his right eye looks plumb into it on one side, and his left eye looks into it on the other. Result is, he can't see nothing at *all!* Now, if he'll only run when he's *blind,* why, we can skin them Socorro people till it seems like a shame.'

"Well, right then we all felt money in our pockets. We seemed most too good to be out ridin' sign, or pullin' old cows out of mudholes. 'You leave all that to me,' says doc. 'By the time I've worked on this patient's nerve centers for a while, I'll make a new horse out of him. You watch me,' says he. That made us all feel cheerful. We thought this wasn't such a bad world, after all.

"We passed the hat in the interest of modern science, and we fenced off a place in the corral and set up a school of ostypathy in our midst. Doc, he done some things that seemed to us right strange at first. He gets pinto up in one corner and takes him by the ear, and tries to break his neck, with his foot in the middle of his back. Then he goes around on the other side and does the same thing. He hammers him up one side and down the other, and works him and wiggles him till us cowpunchers thought he was goin' to scatter him around worse than Cassybianca on the burnin' deck after the exploshun. My experience, though, is that it's right hard to shake a horse to pieces. Pinto, he stood it all right. And say, he got so gentle, with that tall blinder between his eyes, that he'd 'a' followed off a sheepherder.

"All this time we was throwin' oats a-plenty into pinto, rubbin' his legs down, and gettin' him used to a saddle a little bit lighter than a regular cow saddle. Doc, he allows he can see his eyes straightenin' out every day. 'I ought to have a year on this job,' says he; 'but these here is urgent times.'

"I should say they was urgent. The time for the county fair at Socorro was comin' right clost.

"At last we takes the old Hasenberg pinto over to Socorro to the fair, and there we enters him in everything from the front to the back of the racin' book. My friends, you would 'a' shed tears of pity to see them folks fall down over theirselves tryin' to hand us their money against old pinto. There was horses there from Montanny to Arizony, all kinds of fancy riders, and money—oh, law! Us Bar-T fellers, we took everything offered—put up everything we had, down to our spurs. Then we'd go off by ourselves and look at each other solemn. We was gettin' rich so quick we felt almost scared.

"There come nigh to bein' a little shootin' just before the horses was gettin' ready for the first race, which was for a mile and a half. We led old pinto out, and some feller standin' by, he says sarcastic like, 'What's that I see comin'; a snowplow?' Him alludin' to the single blinder on pinto's nose.

"'I reckon you'll think it's been snowin' when we get through,' says Tom Redmond to him, scornful. 'The best thing you can do is to shut up, unless you've got a little money you want to contribute to the Bar-T festerval.' But about then they hollered for the horses to go to the post, and there wasn't no more talk.

"Pinto, he acted meek and humble, just like a glass-eyed angel, and the starter didn't have no trouble with him at all. At last he got them all off, so clost together one saddle blanket would have done for the whole bunch. Say, man, that was a fine start.

"Along with oats and ostypathy, old pinto he'd come out on the track that day just standin' on the edges of his feet, he was feelin' that fine. We put José Santa Maria Trujillo, one of our lightest boys, up on pinto for to ride him. Now a greaser ain't got no sense. It was that fool boy José that busted up modern science on the Bar T.

"I was tellin' you that there horse was ostypathed, so to speak, plumb to a razor edge, and I was sayin' that he went off on a even start. Then what did he do? Run? No, he didn't run. He just sort of passed *away* from the place where he started at. Our greaser, he sees the race is all over, and like any fool cowpuncher, he must get frisky. Comin' down the homestretch, only needin' about one more jump—for it ain't above a quarter of a mile—José, he stands up in his stirrups and pulls off his hat, and just whangs old pinto over the head with it, friendlylike, to show him there ain't no coldness.

"We never did rightly know what happened at that time. The greaser admits he may have busted off the fastenin' of that single blinder down pinto's nose. Anyhow, pinto runs a few short jumps, and then stops, lookin' troubled. The next minute he hides his face on the greaser and there is a glimpse of bright, glad sunlight on the bottom of José's moccasins. Next minute after that pinto is up in the grandstand among the ladies, and there he sits down in the lap of the governor's wife, which was among them present.

"There was time, even then, to lead him down and over the line, but before we could think of that he falls to buckin' sincere and conscientious, up there among the benches, and if he didn't jar his osshus structure a heap *then*, it wasn't no fault of his'n. We all run up in front of the grandstand, and stood lookin' up at pinto, and him the maddest, scaredest, cross-eyedest horse I ever did see in all my life. His single blinder was swingin' loose under his neck. His eyes were right mean and white, and the Mexican saints only knows which way he *was* a-lookin'.

"So there we was," went on Curly, with another sigh, "all Socorro sayin' bright and cheerful things to the Bar T, and us plumb broke, and far, far from home.

"We roped pinto, and led him home behind the wagon, forty miles over the sand, by the soft, silver light of the moon. There wasn't a horse or saddle left in our *rodeo,* and we had to ride on the grub wagon, which you know is a disgrace to any gentleman that wears spurs. Pinto, he was the gayest one in the lot. I reckon he allowed he'd been Queen of the May. Every time he saw a jackrabbit or a bunch of sage brush, he'd snort and take a *pasear* sideways as far as the rope would let him go.

"'The patient seems to be still laborin' under great cerebral excitation,' says the doc, which was likewise on the wagon. 'I ought to have had a year on him,' says he, despondentlike.

"'Shut up,' says Tom Redmond to the doc. 'I'd shoot up your own osshus structure plenty,' he says, 'if I hadn't bet my gun on that horse race.'

"Well, we got home, the wagonload of us, in the mornin' sometime, every one of us ashamed to look the cook in the face, and hopin' the boss was away from home. But he wasn't. He looks at us, and says he, 'Is this a sheep outfit I see before me, or is it the remnants of the former cow camp on the Bar T?' He was right sarcastic. 'Doc,' says he, 'explain this here to me.' But the doc, he couldn't. Says the boss to him at last, 'The *right* time to do the explainin' is before the hoss race is over, and not after,' says he. 'That's the only kind of science that goes hereafter on the Bar T,' says he.

"I reckon the boss was feelin' a little riled, because he had two hundred on pinto hisself. A cross-eyed horse shore can make a sight of trouble," Curly sighed in conclusion, "yet I bought pinto for four dollars and—sometimes, anyway—he's the best horse in my string down at Carrizosy, ain't he, Mac?"

In the thoughtful silence following this tale, Tom Osby knocked his pipe reflectively against a cedar log. "That's the way with the railroad," he said. "It's goin' to come in here with one eye on the gold mines and the other on the town—and there won't be no blind-bridle up in front of Mr. Ingine, neither. If we got as much sense as the Bar-T feller, we'll do our explainin' before, and not after, the hoss race is over. Before I leave for Vegas, I want to see one of you ostypothetic lawyers about that there railroad outfit."

Ranch Truck

by

MIKE LOGAN

A ranch truck's like a rancher.
Don't dress up fit t' kill.
Just goes an' gets the job done
Without no pomp or frill.

While they ain't long on beauty,
Ranch trucks can hold their own.
Just see if this ol' pickup
Don't sound like some you've known.

Me an' Bruce hop in his pickup.
We got some hay to load.
He's got 'er chained on all four wheels
'Cause last night it shore snowed.

Hayhooks festoon the gearshift.
There's stockwhips on the seat.
Ol' Skipper's on the towchains
That's piled beneath my feet.

The windshield's cracked an' muddy.
I give ol' Skip a shove.
The dash wears thirteen mittens
An' one odd left-hand glove.

It also sports three hammers,
Two pairs of fencin' pliers,
A stick 'r two of kindlin'
From last spring's brandin' fires,

Five caps an' some old glasses,
A Pepsi can 'r two,
A box of mixed up nuts an' bolts
An' one old workhorse shoe.

There's binder twine an' ear tags,
Some strings wound on a spool,
A can of pills for calf scours
An' a new ear taggin' tool,

A shot 'r two of Longicil,
A length of rawhide thong,
A pair of ancient channel locks,
A tape just ten feet long,

A crescent wrench, a pill gun,
Band-Aids, a chain saw file,
Three scarves an' one old down vest
All wadded in a pile,

Six washers on a twist of wire,
Eight cents in cold hard cash,
A clevis, a direction book,

An' that's just on the dash.

Between us there's two sacks of cake,
Three jackets an' some chaps,
A slicker an' a Swede saw
An' three new leadrope snaps.

The floor holds one old halter,
An ax, two pairs of spurs,
A head stall an' two oil cans
An' a blanket full of burrs,

Some gunnysacks, a brandin' iron,
A brand new ropin' rope,
A pair of irrigatin' boots
An' a bar of Lava soap.

No tellin' what's behind the seat.
I'm sure ol' Bruce cain't say,
But we won't worry 'bout what's there
'Cause it ain't in the way.

We lost a tally book last week.
I'm 'fraid we're out of luck.
It's prob'ly lost forever
In Bruce's ol' red truck.

Sounds like I'm knockin' Bruce's truck?
Well, that'd be plumb mean.
'Sides, we thought of usin' my rig,
But it ain't half that clean.

A Savage
Santa Claus

by

CHARLES M. RUSSELL

"T ALKIN' ABOUT CHRISTMAS," said Bedrock, as we smoked in his cabin after supper, an' the wind howled as it sometimes can on a blizzardy December night, "puts me in mind of one I spent in the '60s. Me an' a feller named Jake Mason, but better knowed as Beaver, is trappin' an' prospectin' on the head of the Porcupine. We've struck some placer, but she's too cold to work her. The snow's drove all the game out of the country, an' barrin' a few beans and some flour, we're plum out of grub, so we decide we'd better pull our freight before we're snowed in.

"The winter's been pretty open till then, but the day we start there's a storm breaks loose that skins everything I ever seed. It looks like the snow-maker's been holdin' back, an' turned the whole winter supply loose at once. Cold? Well, it would make a polar bear hunt cover.

"About noon it lets up enough so we can see our pack-hosses. We're joggin' along at a good gait, when old Baldy, our lead packhoss, stops an' swings 'round in the trail, bringin' the other three to a stand. His whinner causes me to raise my head, an' lookin' under my hat brim, I'm plenty surprised to see an old log shack not ten feet to the side of the trail.

"'I guess we'd better take that cayuse's advice,' says Beaver, pintin' to Baldy, who's got his ears straightened, lookin' at us as much as to say: 'What, am I packin' fer Pilgrims; or don't you know enough to get in out of the weather? It looks like you'd loosen these packs.' So, takin' Baldy's hunch, we unsaddle.

"This cabin's mighty ancient. It's been two rooms, but the ridge-pole on the rear one's rotted an' let the roof down. The door's wide open an' hangs on a wooden hinge. The animal smell I get on the inside tells me there ain't no humans lived there for many's the winter. The floor's strewn with pine cones an' a few scattered bones, showin' it's been the home of mountain-rats an' squirrels. Takin' it all 'n all, it ain't no palace, but, in this storm, it looks mighty snug, an' when we get a blaze started in the fireplace an' the beans goin' it's comfortable.

"The door to the back's open, an' by the light of the fire I can see the roof hangin' down V-shaped, leavin' quite a little space agin the wall. Once I had a notion of walkin' in an' prospectin' the place, but there's somethin' ghostly about it an' I change my mind.

"When we're rollin' in that night, Beaver asks me what day of the month it is.

"'If I'm right on my dates,' says I, 'this is the evenin' the kids hang up their socks.'

"'The hell it is,' says he. 'Well, here's one camp Santy'll probably overlook. We ain't got no socks nor no place to hang 'em, an' I don't think the old boy'd savvy our foot-rags.' That's the last I remember till I'm waked up along in the night by somethin' monkeyin' with the kettle.

"If it wasn't fer a snufflin' noise I could hear, I'd a-tuk it fer a trade-rat, but with this noise it's no guess with me, an' I call the turn all right, 'cause when I take a peek, there, humped between me an' the fire, is the most robust silvertip I ever see. In size, he resembles a load of hay. The fire's down low, but there's enough light to give me his outline. He's humped over, busy with the beans, snifflin' an' whinin' pleasant, like he enjoys 'em. I nudged Beaver easy, an' whispers: 'Santy Claus is here.'

"He don't need but one look. 'Yes,' says he, reachin' for his Henry, 'but he ain't brought nothin' but trouble, an' more'n a sock full of that. You couldn't crowd it into a wagon-box.'

"This whisperin' disturbs Mr. Bear, an' he straightens up till he near touches the ridge-pole. He looks eight feet tall. Am I scared? Well, I'd tell a man. By the feelin' runnin' up and down my back, if I had bristles I'd resemble a wild hog. The cold sweat's drippin' off my nose, an' I ain't got nothin' on me but sluice-ice.

"The bark of Beaver's Henry brings me out of this scare. The bear goes over, upsettin' a kettle of water, puttin' the fire out. If it wasn't for a stream of fire runnin' from Beaver's weapon, we'd be in plumb darkness. The bear's up agin, bellerin' an' bawlin', and comin' at us mighty warlike, and by the time I get my Sharp's workin', I'm near choked with smoke. It's the noisiest muss I was ever mixed up in. Between the smoke, the barkin' of the guns an' the bellerin' of the bear, it's like hell on a holiday.

"I'm gropin' for another ca'tridge when I hear the lock on Beaver's gun click, an' I know his magazine's dry. Lowerin' my hot gun, I listen. Everythin's quiet now. In the sudden stillness I can hear the drippin' of blood. It's the bear's life runnin' out.

"'I guess it's all over,' says Beaver, kind of shaky. 'It was a short fight, but a fast one, an' hell was poppin' while she lasted.'

"When we get the fire lit, we take a look at the battle ground. There lays Mr. Bear in a ring of blood, with a hide so full of holes he wouldn't hold hay. I don't think there's a bullet went 'round him.

"This excitement wakens us so we don't sleep no more that night. We breakfast on bear meat. He's an old bear an' it's pretty stout, but a feller livin' on beans and bannocks straight for a couple of weeks don't kick much on flavor, an' we're at a stage where meat's meat.

"When it comes day, me an' Beaver goes lookin' over the bear's bedroom. You know, daylight drives away ha'nts, an' this room don't look near so ghostly as it did last night. After winnin' this fight, we're both mighty brave. The roof caved in with four or five feet of snow on, makes the rear room still dark, so, lightin' a pitch-pine glow, we start explorin'.

"The first thing we bump into is the bear's bunk. There's a rusty pick layin' up against the wall, an' a gold-pan on the floor, showin' us that the human that lived there was a miner. On the other side of the shack we ran onto a pole bunk, with a weather-wrinkled buffalo robe an' some rotten blankets. The way the roof slants, we can't see into the bed, but by usin' an axe an' choppin' the legs off, we lower it to view. When Beaver raises the light, there's the frame-work of a man. He's layin' on his left side, like he's sleepin', an' looks like he cashed in easy. Across the bunk, under his head, is an old-fashioned cap-'n-ball rifle. On the bedpost hangs a powder horn an' pouch, with a belt an' skinnin' knife. These things tell us that this man's a pretty old-timer.

"Findin' the pick an' gold-pan causes us to look more careful for what he'd been diggin'. We explore the bunk from top to bottom, but nary a find. All day long we prospects. That evenin', when we're fillin' up on bear meat, beans and bannocks, Beaver says he's goin' to go through the bear's bunk; so, after we smoke, relightin' our torches, we start our search again.

"Sizin' up the bear's nest, we see he'd laid there quite a while. It looks like Mr. Silvertip, when the weather gets cold, starts huntin' a winter location for his long snooze. Runnin' onto this cabin, vacant, and lookin' like it's for rent, he jumps the claim an' would have been snoozin' there yet, but our fire warmin' up the place fools him. He thinks it's spring an' steps out to look at the weather. On the way he strikes this breakfast of beans, an' they hold him till we object.

"We're lookin' over this nest when somethin' catches my eye on the edge of the waller. It's a hole, roofed over with willers.

"'Well, I'll be damned. There's his cache,' says Beaver, whose eyes has follered mine. It don't take a minute to kick these willers loose, an' there lays a buckskin sack with five hundred dollars in dust in it.

"'Old Santy Claus, out there,' says Beaver, pointin' to the bear through the door, 'didn't load our socks, but he brought plenty of meat an' showed us the cache, for we'd never a-found it if he hadn't raised the lid.'

"The day after Christmas we buried the bones, wrapped in one of our blankets, where we'd found the cache. It was the best we could do.

"'I guess the dust's ours,' says Beaver. 'There's no papers to show who's his kin-folks.' So we splits the pile an' leaves him sleepin' in the tomb he built for himself."

It Was Just a Habit

by

WILL ROGERS

IN ALL THE AUTOBOGRAPHYS I ever read the first line was I was born at So-and-so on Such-and-such a Date. That is the accustomed first line of any Autubiography. Now the thing that struck me was if a fellow could give a reason why he was born you'd be a novelty. Now that is what has been holding me up on this Autobography, I was born, but why? Now I've got it.

I was born because it was a habit in those days, people dident know anything else. In those days they dident put a Bounty on you for being born. Nowadays, the income Tax allows you 200 dollars for each child. Just removing his adanoids cost more than that, to say nothing about his food, Tonsils and Fraternoty pins. In those days a Doctor would bring you into the World for two Dollars a visit and make good money at it. Everything you was born with was supposed to be buried with you, but nowadays when you die about all you have left at the funeral is Scars and stitches.

If you had the stomack Ache the Doctor cured it; if you have it nowadays they remove it.

Ether has replaced pills as our national commodity.

So I just figured out I was born as a Martyr to the ignorance of old time Drs. It was the law of averages that put me here. I beat

Race Suicide by just one year, I arrived when childbirth was not grounds for divorce. If a family dident have at least 8 children in those days the Father was either in jail or deceased.

MOTHER and Baby doing well was our National yell.

It falls to the lot of few to be born on National Holidays. A Child born on the Fourth of July, as my good friend George Cohan was, has to spend the rest of his life waving a flag. A child born on Xmas uses the Chimney for an entrance even after he is married. The New Years child arrived with wonderful resolutions and passes out by electrocution.

I am the only known child in History who claims Nov. 4th as my Birthday, that is election day. Women couldent vote in those days so My Mother thought she would do something, so she stayed home and gave birth to me. The men were all away. I decided to get even with the Government. Thats why I have always had it in for politicians.

I was the only child born on our beat that day. The news had to cross the Country by Pony Express, so it was two years later that it reached Washington, so Garfield was shot.

I was born on the Verdigris river, one mile below where Spencer Creek enters the river. Rutherford B. Hayes was President at the time of my birth.

I was the youngest and last of 7 Children. My folks looked me over and instead of the usual drowning procedure, they said, "This thing has gone far enough, if they are going to look like this, we will stop."

I was born at our old Ranch 12 miles north of Claremore, Okla (the home of the best Radium Water in the World). It was a big two story Log House, but on the back we had three rooms made of frame. Just before my birth my mother, being in one of these frame rooms, had them remove her into the Log part of the House. She wanted me to be born in a log House. She had just read the life of Lincoln. So I got the Log house end of it OK. All I need now is the other qualifications.

It is customary in most Auto biographies to devote a couple of paragraphs to the parents. Now in my case the parents should have the Article devoted to them and the couple of Paragraphs to me.

My father was Clem V. Rogers, a Part Cherokee Indian, who was a Captain under Stan Waitie during the Civil War. He afterwards freighted from St Joe, Mo., to Dallas, Texas. The Covered Wagon went West and got into Pictures. He went South. If he had gone West instead of South, he might have got into "The Covered Wagon," or maybe the "10 Commandments."

He did that for years until he found out that St. Joe, Missouri, dident have anything that Dallas, Texas dident have (outside of the James Boys). Under the circumstances I think my Father was pretty wise in quitting hauling from St. Joe to Dallas. He went into the Cattle Business and settled on the Ranch we have in the family yet. They drove a bunch of Cattle from down there up to Kansas City, and unlike the Story of North of 36, there was no Girl with the outfit, no Negro Maids. They just took Cattle. Well, when they got to KC they couldent sell them. There was no celebration when they drove into town, so they said what other Town have you got around here that want 3 thousand cattle. They said, why St. Louis, Lemp and Anhauser Busch had just moved into St. Louis so Papa and his gang lit out for there, only 590 miles. Now if I wanted to make a scenario out of this instead of the truth, I would tell you that they couldent sell in St. Louis and had to go on to Chicago, but such is not the truth. They dident happen to meet any one with a sense of humor to tell em that. They only lost one Steer. He jumped off the Boat crossing the Mississippi going over to East St. Louis and tried to swim back to Missouri. He really committed suicide rather than enter Illinois. He went on down the river and I dont know at that if he ever drowned. Mark Twain just liable to picked him up with one of those Mississippi Steam shovels of his, on down the river some place. Then they all had to ride back home to the Indian Territory Horseback. They dident by the way have to go back by KC. Jim Reed had just begin practicing law there in KC then and they knew that he would figure out some way to take this money away from them.

Papa rode a Mule on the whole trip, not much romance in that, thats why he come back single.

Mamas name was Mary and if your Mother was an old-fashioned Woman and named Mary you dont need to say much for her, everybody knows already.

Most men in their Auto Biographies after they are born kinder skip over a lapse of time, and they dont seem to be able to remember anything until they get up able to hold political office. Now that is the only thing remarkable about me, I looked em all over the next day after arrival and sized the whole thing up and says this Life is going to be a lot of Apple Sauce. Being born on election day, it kinder gave me the advantage of seeing the Bunk in it all. I arrived amid a day of crooked Ballotts. I could read when I was a year old. I was not a Child Prodigy, because a Child Prodigy is a child who knows as much when it is a Child as it does when it grows up.

Well, the next year, 1880, why Garfield was elected President on my first Birthday. I dident vote but they voted my name every year up to 18.

The East River in NY froze over that year and people walked over without paying Subway fare. Garfield was Assassinated in a Depot in Washington waiting for the Baltimore and Ohio Railroad train. He is the first man ever assassinated waiting for one of those trains but he is not the first casualty, as thousands have starved to death waiting for em. I can remember the day of the Assassination. I cried that day, well I cried the day before and the day after too, but I remember that particular day well.

I was named by an Indian Chief, William Penn Adair. He says, "Mary, I want another young Chief named for me. I name him Will Penn Adair Rogers." The River was up and he had to stay there a week, so he got paid for his name. I just looked at him when he named me and thought by the time I get to be big enough to be Chief we wont have any more Country than a Jay Bird.

All Auto Biographies have pictures of the person being auto-bied. Now I have some taken at the age of three in a group at a Circus. Of course I havent got many with prominent men taken at the opportune time because at that time I did not know that I would ever have an Autobiography.

Well, Claremore is the county seat of Rogers County, which was named for my father. My family had lived there for over fifty years. My father was one-eighth Cherokee Indian and my mother was a quarter-blood Cherokee. I never got far enough in arithmetic to figure out just how much "Injun" that makes me, but there's nothing of which I am more proud than my Cherokee blood. My father was a senator in the tribe for years, and was a member of the convention that drafted the constitution of the State of Oklahoma.

My father was pretty well fixed, and I being the only male son he tried terribly hard to make something out of me. He sent me to about every school in that part of the country. In some of them I would last for three or four months. I got just as far as the fourth reader when the teachers wouldn't seem to be running the school right, and rather than have the school stop I would generally leave.

Then I would start in at another school, tell them I had just finished the third reader and was ready for the fourth. Well, I knew all this fourth grade by heart, so the teacher would remark:

"I never see you studying, yet you seem to know your lessons." I had that education thing figured down to a fine point. Three years in McGuffey's Fourth Reader, and I knew more about it than McGuffey did.

But I don't want any enterprising youth to get the idea that I had the right dope on it. I have regretted all my life that I did not at least take a chance on the fifth grade. It would certainly come in handy right now, and I never go through a day that I am not sorry for the idea I had of how to go to school and not learn anything.

I was just a thinking what I would have to do if I was to start out to help out my old schools. "Drumgoul" was a little one-room log cabin four miles east of Chelsea, Indian Territory (where I am right now writing). It was all Indian kids went there and I being part Cherokee had enough white in me to make my honesty questionable.

There must have been about thirty of us in that room that had rode horseback and walked miles to get there, and by the way it was a Co Ed Institution. About half of em was Coo-Coo Eds. We graduated when we could print our full names and enumerate to the teacher, or Principle or Faculty (well, whenever we could name to her), the nationality of the last Democratic President.

But as I say the school went out of business. We wasent able to get games which was profitable. It seems that other school grabbed off all the other good dates, and got the breaks in the newspapers. We couldent seem to ever be accused of professionalism. I could see the finish even as far back as when I was there along in 1887.

Why I can remember when the Coach couldent get enough out of us 15 Boys out to make a team. We got to running Horse Races instead. I had a little chestnut mare that was beating everything that any of them could ride to school and I was losing interest in what we was really there for. I was kinder forgetting that we was there to put the old school on a Paying basis by seeing how many times we could get through that Goal with that old pigskin.

I got to thinking well Horseracing is the big game, thats where the money is, thats what the crowds pay to see. But as years went along it showed that I was a Lad of mighty poor foresight. Little did I dream that it was football that was to be the real McCoy. Course we had no way of hardly telling it then, for we was paid practically nothing at all. In fact we had what I would call a Real Simon Pure Amateur Team. Course we got our side line (Schooling) free. The Cherokee Nation (we then had our own Government and the name Oklahoma was as foreign to us as a Tooth Paste), well, the Cherokee Nation paid the Teacher.

But anyhow there was a mighty few of us that was there under any kind of a guarantee. Course I will admit one of the Alumni got me to go there. He had spent three weeks there and couldent get along with the Teacher and he wanted to do what he could for the old School so he procured me. I looked like a promising End. I could run pretty fast. In fact my nickname was and is to this day among some of the old-timers "Rabbit." I could never figure out if that referred to my speed or my heart.

Mind you, you wouldent believe it, but we dident even have a Stadium. Think of that in this day and time! Thousands and Thousands of acres surrounded us with not a thing on it but Cows and not a concrete seat for a spectator to sit on. Well you see as I look back on it now, a school like that dident have any license to exist. It had to perish. It just staid with books such as Rays Arithmetic and McGuffy 1st, 2nd, and 2 pupils in the 3rd Readers. We had a Geography around there but we just used it for the pictures of the cattle grazing in the Argentine and the wolves attacking the sleighs in Russia.

Well you see they just couldent see what was the future in Colleges. They just wore out the old books instead of wearing out some footballs. We had Indian Boys that could knock a Squirrel out of a Tree with a rock. But do you think the Regents knew enough to get a Pop Warner and teach em how to hide a Ball under their Jerseys? No. They just had the old-fashioned idea that the place must be made self-sustaining by learning alone, and you see where their ignorance got them. Now the weeds is higher there than the School house was and thats what is happening in a few places in this country. We got those same "Drumgoul" ideas. Course not many but a few. They wont switch and get to the new ideas that its open field running that gets your old College somewhere and not a pack of spectacled Orators or a mess of Civil Engineers. Its better to turn out one good Coach than Ten College Presidents. His name will be in the papers every day and it will always be referred to where he come from. But with the College Presidents, why as far as publicity is concerned they just as well might have matriculated in Hong Kong. So dont let your school be another Drumgoul.

Well, back to my autobography. You see, the lariat-slinging business drifted into my system when I was pretty young. My father would send me out on the ranch, but instead of riding the range I'd go off into a shady place and there spend the time practicing with the rope—cutting curliques and things in the prairie breeze or lassoing prairie dogs and things not made to be lassoed.

Then he hired me out to other ranch-men, but I was so fond of using the lariat when there was no call for it that I couldn't hold a job. In a fit of bad temper the old gent decided to make a preacher of me, and he sent me to a school up in Missouri. When I lassoed the stone gal—goddess of something—off the top of the water fountain and broke all her limbs, the old gent paid the bill rather than have me sent back to the nation, because he didn't need me on the ranch, but when I got the string around the Professor's neck—by accident—my career on the road to the ministry ended.

My old daddy—Uncle Clem, they called him—then sent me to a military school at Boonville, Mo., Kemper, thinking the discipline might tame me.

Will arrived there on January 13, 1897, dressed in a ten-gallon hat, with a braided horsehair cord, flannel shirt with a red bandana handkerchief, highly colored vest, and high-heeled red top boots with spurs and his trousers legs tucked in the boot tops. He carried coiled ropes outside his luggage.

Me and Ben Johnson, down at Chickasha, Oklahoma, were buddies together at Kemper, just a couple of poor ornery Indian boys. But the fact is we were sent to the Missouri State reformatory which is located near the same town and through somebody's mistake, they enrolled us at the Kemper Military Academy instead.

Col. Johnson—the head man—didn't run Kemper in accordance with the standards that I thought befitting a growing intellect. I was spending my third year in the fourth grade and wasn't being appreciated, so I not only left them flat during a dark night, but quit the entire school business for life.

Billy Johnston of Canadian, Texas, was also an inmate, and a ranch boy like I had been in Oklahoma, so he advised me of a friend's ranch at Higgins, Texas. I, not wanting to face my father with what little I knew, lit a shuck for there.

When I got there, the outfit had gone away, boss and all. Just a cook and two or three old broke-down cowboys was left.

I stayed around until the boss, Mr. Ewing, and his son Frank came back and they give me a job. We took a trail herd to Kansas and I worked with them for some time. He was a great fellow, funny as they make em. I got enough money to buy me an old horse and lit out for Amarillo, Texas.

This country was thinly settled then—only passed three ranches on the way in. They'd let me cook up a lot of biscuits and some jerky—dried beef—and then that old skate and I would amble on.

One night I staked him out in good grass and hit the old sougans, as I was dead tired. During the night a thunder storm come up. I'd never seen such lightning and heard such noise in my life. A big bunch of range horses got frightened and run smack into that rope I'd staked my old horse out with. When it come another flash of lightning, I couldent see him and thought he'd been killed.

I was wet as a drowned rat and hit out back for a line camp I'd passed and hadn't gone in. I knocked and yelled, "Hello! Hello!" and nobody answered. I went in and as my matches was all wet—fumbled around in the dark till I found a table and went to sleep on it. When I woke the sun was shining bright and there just six feet away was a good warm bunk with blankets and everything. There was coffee and a side of bacon and I made a fire in the stove and cooked up a bait. After I got the wrinkles out of my belly I lit out on foot. About a mile from the camp I went up on a little hill and there on the other side was my horse grazing away on the grass as good as ever.

When I finally got into Amarillo the whole country around was covered with trail herds waiting for cars to ship them away. There was plenty of grass and water everywhere.

I hit up every trail boss I could find for a job, but they didn't want me. At night I'd go out a piece from town, stake out my horse, and sleep, then the next morning go back.

While I dident have anything else to do, I got to watching an old spotted dog. He was just an ordinary dog, but when I looked at him close, he was alert and friendly with everyone. Got to inquiring around and found out he'd been bumped off a freight train and seemed to have no owner. He made himself at home and started right in business. When a crowd of cowboys would go into a saloon, he would follow em in and begin entertaining. He could do all kinds of tricks—turn somersaults, lay down and roll over, sit up on his hind feet, and such like.

He would always rush to the door and shake hands with all the newcomers. The boys would lay a coin on his nose, and he'd toss it high in the air and catch it in his mouth and pretend to swallow it. But you could bet your life he dident swallow it—he stuck it in one side of his lip and when he got a lip full of money, he'd dash out the back door and disappear for a few minutes. What he really done was hide his money. As soon as he worked one saloon, he would pull out and go to another place.

I got to thinking while watching this old dog, how much smarter he is than me. Here I am out of a job five hundred miles from home, and setting around and cant find a thing to do, and this old dog hops off a train and starts right in making money, hand over fist.

Me and some boys around town tried to locate his hidden treasure, but this old dog was too slick for us. He never fooled away no time on three or four of us boys that was looking for work. He seemed to know we was broke, but he was very friendly. As he was passing along by me, he'd wag his tail and kinda wink. I must a looked hungry and forlorn. I think he wanted to buy me a meal.

When times was dull and he got hungry, he would mysteriously disappear. Pretty soon he'd show up at a butcher shop with a dime in his mouth and lay it on the counter and the butcher would give him a piece of steak or a bone. He always paid for what he got in the line of grub. Pretty soon he seemed to get tired of the town, and one morning he was gone. A railroad man told us later that he seen this same dog in Trinidad, Colorado.

One morning a merchant told me a trail boss had sent him word to hire him a hand, but that he already spoke to another boy. He told me to go see him just in case he dident want the other boy. I was on the spot, you bet.

Right then I seen a feller talk himself out of a job. He started in telling the boss what a good hand he was. The old cowman listened to him till he had had his say, then he told him, "I'm in need of a hand all right, but I think you'd suit me too well."

I just told him maby I could do the work. He told me to get on my horse and come out to his camp. Them was the happiest words I ever heard in my life.

I got to the chuck wagon just in time for dinner. The boys setting around grinned as I stowed away helping after helping of beans. But when I finished there wasent a wrinkle left in my belly.

The boss put me to wrangling ponies. We moved on up to Panhandle City crossing the Canadian River at a Famous Ranch, where Remington had painted some of his pictures, the old "L.X." Ranch. We went on over to the boss' ranch near Woodward, Oklahoma, where I worked through the roundup and helped brand the calves.

Finally, I got tired and another boy and I went to California with a shipment of cattle and up to Frisco, and that night something happened. He says he didn't blow the gas out, maybe there was a leak. I was asleep when he came in—anyhow they dug us out of there next morning and hauled us to a hospital, and believe me I didn't know a fighting thing until late that night and that was just bull luck. The main doctors game me up, but a lot of young medical students just by practicing on me happened to light on some nut remedy that no regular doctor would ever think of and I come alive.

Well I landed back home pretty badly buggered up. This stuff had located in my system. I went to Hot Springs to boil it out and when I would get in a hot room they would all think the gas was escaping some place.

Well, my old dad called me off a few weeks later and told me, "If you're bound to punch cows, there's no need for you to leave home. You're the only child I have at home now, as your sisters are married and have homes of their own, I'm a going to give you this Dog Iron Ranch, lock, stock and barrel. It's yours and you can run it the way you want to, for I'm going to move to Claremore."

Well, I dident exactly run it to suit him. I danced all my young life to the music of old country fiddlers and I dident drag a bad bow myself. Between dances and roping contests, I dident have time for much serious ranching business.

I had a little cream-colored pony with a white mane and tail, named Comanche. He was about the best horse wrapped up in that much hide. I used to race horses with some Negroes lived next to us. One of the boys owned his horse. Couldent ever beat him so swapped him my horse and ten dollars to boot for him.

Well, I remember when we was out at a steer roping and bronc busting contest at the Elks' Carnival at Springfield, Missouri. A cowboy that I let ride Comanche roped a steer and threw him right in front of the grand stand. When he jumped off to tie the steer, the old cuss rolled over and got to his feet and charged straight at him, cutting him off from his horse. But old Comanche, when the steer crossed the rope, turned and busted him all by himself. The cowboy dident lose over three seconds time in tying him.

A wealthy New Yorker come down from the grandstand and wanted to buy the pony. He finally got up to five hundred dollars. "A dollar looks as big to me as a wagon wheel," I told him, "but I just don't want to sell him."

He came back, "He can be bought for some price, name it, and I'll ship him to Long Island, New York."

"Mister," I told him, "I don't know how much money you got, but there ain't money enough in that grand stand to buy old Comanche."

Well, I kept going to these steer-roping contests. I learned a lot from men like Clay McGonagill, Tom Vest, Abe Wilson, and the rest of the top-notchers who'd be there. Shortly after the Spanish-American War, the Rough Riders held a reunion at Oklahoma City. When I got there the fair grounds was full of horses and cowboys. These contestants were cowboys right off the ranches that done roping work every day. They come from Texas, New Mexico, Arizona, Colorado, Wyoming, and, of course, Indian Territory.

Colonel Theodore Roosevelt was there, mixing in with us boys. Old Booger Red was there from San Angelo, Texas. I broke my rope and old Jim O'Donnell won. He'd of beat me anyhow.

My real show career kinder dates from the time I first run into the Col. Zack Mulhall. It was in 1899 at the St. Louis fair (not the Worlds fair) just the big St. Louis fair they held every year. They had decided as an attraction that they would put on a Roping and Riding Contest. They were not called Rodeo's or Stampedes, in those days they were just what they are, a "Roping and Riding Contest." Well I was pretty much of a Kid, but had just happened to have won the first and about my only Contest at home in Claremore, Okla., and then we read about them wanting entries for this big contest at St. Louis.

Well some one sent in my name, and the first thing I knew I was getting transportaton for myself and pony to the affair. Well I went, and Col. Zack Mulhall had charge of it. I dident get very far in this St. Louis Contest. I made the serious mistake of catching my steer and he immediately jerked me and my Pony down for our trouble.

But that gave me a touch of "Show business" in a way, so that meant I was ruined for life as far as actual employment was concerned. He had a couple of Daughters, Miss "Bossy" and Lucille. Bossy was quite a good rider but she never took it up in the professional way that little Lucille did. Lucille was just a little kid when we were in St. Louis that year, but she was riding and running her Pony all over the place, and that was incidentally her start too. It was not only her start, but it was the direct start of what has since come to be known as the Cowgirl. There was no such a thing or no such word then as Cowgirl. But as Col. Mulhall from that date drifted into the professional end of the Contest and show business, why Lucille gradually come to the front, and you can go tell the world that his youngest Daughter Lucille Mulhall was the first well-known Cowgirl.

She become a very expert roper, and was the first girl that could rope and tie a Steer, not only do it but do it in such time that it would make a good roper hustle to beat her.

Colonel Mulhall was at the time general stock agent for the Frisco Railroad. He got together a Cowboy Band of about sixty musicians. They was dressed in ten-gallon hats, jackets, chaps, boots and spurs. We made all the State Fairs through the Middle West. As those musicians could not ride in a wagon unless their shirt tails was nailed to the floor, Colonel Zack thought it would help to have a few cowboys along.

He advertised he could pick out boys in the band that would ride any old outlaw horse in the State. He offered to bet that we could rope and tie a steer in less time than anybody they could produce. Me and Jim O'Donnell had to produce—mostly Jim. There we'd sit with the band, me with a trombone which I couldn't make a sound on.

Well, once we got invited down to the Fair at San Antone. That time we needed help so we wired old Clay McGonagill and little Joe Gardener. It wasent like it is now—a little runty calf. You roped steers. Them big boogers was given a hundred foot start and when the flag dropped, the roper's rope was tied to his saddle. All he had to do was to take down his rope, build a loop, rope the steer, throw him and tie his legs. When you finished, you held up your hands. In ten minutes, the judge would look that steer over and if he was still tied properly, you got your time. You had to tie em good and tight. The judge was old John Blocker, who knew more about a calf than her mother did. Boy, we sure needed old Clay and Joe that time.

Those Texas folks liked our band and took us in. They give us the town. Then they had a barbecue for us and while I was stacking in the grub, someone asked me to speak. I guess I sorter blinked and scratched my head and finally stammered, "Well, folks, this is a mighty fine dinner, what there is of it." That surprised them and me too. I saw I wasent going so good, so I said, trying to cover up, "Well, there is plenty of it, such as it is."

Maby that was my first after-dinner speech because that was all there was of it.

We had a lot of visitors at the Mulhall and amongst them once was a big raw-boned Irishman. He was the sheriff of Marshall, Oklahoma. The election was coming up soon, so he decided to give a big barbecue at Bart Murphy's Ranch. As he was a great friend of Col. Mulhall, we decided to go over and put on a show for him.

Well, when we got there it looked like everybody that lived in the country was there to spend the night. The barns and corrals was all filled with horses and mules, and the house was crammed full of women. All the men had to sleep out of doors, or in the barns.

When we left camp, there wasn't much money amongst any of us. Tom Mix and I had five dollars between us. We couldn't get change and, as you'd suspect, it was in Tom's pants. It was hot and Tom pulled off his pants. During the night, those pants and my hat fell down into a stall where there was a big old Missouri mule. He et both of em. The next morning I went bareheaded and Tom had nothing to wear but his chaps. Guess that old mule digested that five dollars, we dident spend it. Anyhow, we had a big day with a barbecue and danced that night till three o'clock. I dont remember, but I'll bet that big Irishman was re-elected sheriff.

How Jack Rainey Quit

by

ALFRED HENRY LEWIS

"C USTOMARY, we has our social round-ups in the Red Light," observed the Old Cattleman; "which I mentions once it does us for a club. We're all garnered into said fold that time when Dave Tutt tells us how this yere Jack Rainey quits out.

"'Rainey gets downed,' says Tutt, 'mainly because his system's obscoore, an' it chances that a stranger who finds himse'f immeshed tharin takes it plumb ombrageous; an' pendin' explanations, gets tangled up with a pard of Rainey's, goes to a gun play, an' all accidental an' casooal Rainey wings his way to them regions of the blest.

"'Now I allers holds,' goes on Tutt, 'an' still swings an' rattles with that decision, that it's manners to ask strangers to drink; an' that no gent, onless he's a sky-pilot or possesses scrooples otherwise, has a right to refoose. Much less has a gent, bein' thus s'licited to licker, any license to take it hostile an' allow he's insulted, an' lay for his entertainers with weepons.'

"'Well, I don't know, neither,' says Texas Thompson, who's a heap dispootatious an' allers spraddlin' in on every chance for an argyment. 'Thar's a party, now deceased a whole lot—the Stranglers over in Socorro sort o' chaperones this yere gent to a cottonwood an' excloodes the air from his lungs with a lariat for mebby it's an hour—an' this party I'm alloodin' at, which his name is Flowler, is plumb murderous. Now, it's frequent with him when he's selected a victim that a-way, an' while he's bickerin' with him up to the killin' p'int, to invite said sacrifice to take a drink. When they're ag'inst the bar, this yere Fowler we-all strangles would pour out a glass of whiskey an' chuck it in the eyes of that onfortunate he's out to down. Of course, while this party's blind with the nose-paint, he's easy; an' Fowler tharupon c'llects his skelp in manner, form an' time to suit his tastes. Now I takes it that manners don't insist none on no gent frontin' up to a bar on the invite of sech felons as Fowler, when a drink that a-way means a speshul short-cut to the tomb.'

"'All this yere may be troo,' replies Tutt, 'but it's a exception. What I insists is, Texas, that speakin' wide an' free an' not allowin' none for sports of the Fowler brand, it's manners to ask strangers to stand in on what beverages is goin'; an' that it's likewise manners for said strangers to accept; an' it shows that both sides concerned tharin is well brought up by their folks. Sech p'liteness is manners, goin' an' comin', which brings me with graceful swoops back to how Jack Rainey gets shot up.'

"'But, after all,' breaks in Texas ag'in, for he feels wranglesome, 'manners is frequent a question of where you be. What's manners in St. Looey may be bad jedgment in Texas; same as some commoonities plays straights in poker, while thar's regions where straights is barred.'

"'Texas is dead right about his State that a-way,' says Jack Moore, who's heedin' of the talk. 'Manners is a heap more inex'rable in Texas than other places. I recalls how I'm galivantin' 'round in the Panhandle country—it's years ago when I'm young an' recent—an' as I'm ridin' along south of the Canadian one day, I discerns a pony an' a gent an' a fire, an' what looks like a yearlin' calf tied down. I knows the pony for Lem Woodruff's cayouse, an' heads over to say "Howdy" to Lem. He's about half a mile away; when of a sudden he stands up—he's been bendin' over the yearlin' with a runnin' iron in his hand—an' gives a whoop an' makes some copious references towards me with his hands. I wonders what for a game he's puttin' up, an' whatever is all this yere sign-language likely to mean; but I keeps ridin' for'ard. It's then this Woodruff steps over to his pony, an' takin' his Winchester off the saddle, cuts down with it in my direction, an' onhooks her—"Bang!" The bullet raises the dust over about fifty yards to the right. Nacherally I pulls up my pony to consider conduct. While I'm settin' thar tryin' to fig-ger out Woodruff's system, thar goes that Winchester ag'in' an' a streak of dust lifts up, say fifty yards to the left. I then sees Lem objects to me. I don't like no gent to go carpin' an' criticisin' at me with a gun; but havin' a Winchester that a-way, this yere Woodruff can overplay me with only a six-shooter, so I quits him an' rides contemptuous away. As I withdraws, he hangs his rifle on his sad-dle ag'in' picks up his runnin' iron an' goes back content an' all serene to his maverick.'"

"What is a maverick?" I asked, interrupting my friend in the flow of his narration.

"Why, I s'posed," he remarked, a bit testily at being halted, "as how even shorthorns an' tender-feet knows what mavericks is. Mav-ericks, son, is calves which gets sep'rated from the old cows, their mothers, an' ain't been branded none yet. They're bets which the round-ups overlooks, an' don't get marked. Of course, when they drifts from their mothers, each calf for himse'f, an' no brands nor y'ear marks, no one can tell whose calves they be. They ain't brand-ed, an' the old cows ain't thar to identify an' endorse 'em, an' thar you stands in ignorance. Them's mavericks.

"It all comes," he continued in further elucidation of mavericks, "when cattle brands is first invented in Texas. The owners, whose cattle is all mixed up on the ranges, calls a meetin' to decide on brands, so each gent'll know his own when he crosses up with it, an' won't get to burnin' powder with his neighbors over a steer which breeds an' fosters doubts. After every party announces what his brand an' y'ear mark will be, an' the same is put down in the book, a old longhorn named Maverick addresses the meetin', an' puts it up if so be thar's no objection, now they all has brands but him, he'll let his cattle lope without markin', an' every gent'll savcy said Maverick's cattle because they won't have no brand. Cattle without brands, that a-way, is to belong to Maverick, that's the scheme, an' as no one sees no reason why not, they lets old Maverick's proposal go as it lays.

"An' to cut her short, for obv'ous reasons, it ain't no time before Maverick, claimin' all the onbranded cattle, has herds on herds of 'em; whereas thar's good authority which states that when he makes his bluff about not havin' no brand that time, all the cattle old Maverick has is a triflin' bunch of Mexican steers an' no semblances of cows in his outfit. From which onpromisin', not to say barren, beginnin', Maverick owns thousands of cattle at the end of ten years. It all provokes a heap of merriment an' scorn. An' ever since that day, onmarked an onbranded cattle is called 'mavericks.' But to go back ag'in to what Jack Moore is remarkin' about this yere outlaw, Woodruff, who's been bustin' away towards Jack with his Winchester.

"'It's a week later,' goes on Jack Moore, 'when I encounters this sport Woodruff in Howard's store over in Tascosa. I stands him up an' asks whatever he's shootin' me up for that day near the Serrita la Cruz.

""Which I never sees you nohow," replies this yere Woodruff, laughin'. "I never cuts down on you with no Winchester, for if I did, I'd got you a whole lot. You bein' yere all petulant an' irritated is mighty good proof I never is shootin' none at you. But bein' you're new to the Canadian country an' to Texas, let me give you a few p'inters on cow ettyquette an' range manners. Whenever you notes a gent afar off with a fire goin' an' a yearlin' throwed an' hawg-tied ready to mark up a heap with his own private hieroglyphics, don't you-all go pesterin' 'round him. He ain't good company, sech a gent ain't. Don't go near him. It's ag'in the law in Texas to brand calves lonely an' forlorn that a-way, without stoppin' to herd 'em over to some well-known corral, an' the punishment it threatens, bein' several years in Huntsville, makes a gent when he's violatin' it a heap misanthropic, an' he don't hunger none for folks to come ridin' up to see about whatever he reckons he's at. Mebby later them visitors gets roped up before a co't, or jury, to tell whatever they may know. So, as I says, an' merely statin' a great trooth in Texas ettyquette, yereafter on beholdin' a fellow-bein' with a calf laid out to make, don't go near him a little bit. It's manners to turn your back onto him an' ignore him plumb severe. He's a crim'nal, an' any se'f-respectin' gent is jestified in refoosin' to affiliate with him. Wherefore, you ride away from every outcast you tracks up ag'inst who is engaged like you says this onknown party is the day he fetches loose his Winchester at you over by the Serrita la Cruz."

"'That's what this Woodruff says,' concloodes Jack, windin' up his interruption, 'about what's manners in Texas; an' when it's made explicit that a-way, I sees the force of his p'sition. Woodruff an' me buys nose-paint for each other, shakes hearty, an' drops the discussion. But it shorely comes to this: manners, as Texas declar's, is sometimes born of geography, an' what goes for polish an' the p'lite play in St. Looey may not do none for Texas.'

"'Mighty likely,' says Old Man Enright, 'what Texas Thompson an' Jack Moore interjecks yere is dead c'rrect; but after all this question about what's manners is 'way to one side of the main trail. I tharfore su'gests at this crisis that Black Jack do his best with a bottle, an' when every gent has got his p'ison, Dave Tutt proceeds for'ard with the killin' of this Jack Rainey.'

"'Goin' on as to said Rainey,' observes Tutt, followin' them remarks of Enright, 'as I explains when Texas an' Moore runs me down with them interestin' outbreaks, Rainey gets ag'inst it over in a jimcrow camp called Lido; an' this yere is a long spell ago.

"'Rainey turns in an' charters every bar in Lido, an' gets his brand onto all the nose-paint. He's out to give the camp an orgy, an' not a gent can spend a splinter or lose a chip to any bar for a week. Them's Jack Rainey's commands. A sport orders his forty drops, an' the barkeep pricks it onto a tab; at the end of a week Jack Rainey settles all along the line, an' the "saturnalia," as historians calls 'em, is over. I might add that Jack Rainey gives way to these yere charities once a year, an the camp of Lido is plumb used tharto an' approves tharof.

"'On this sad o'casin when Jack Rainey gets killed, this yere excellent custom he invents is in full swing. Thar's notices printed plenty big, an' posted up in every drink-shop from the dance hall to the Sunflower saloon; which they reads as follows:

RUIN! RUIN! RUIN!

CUT LOOSE!

JACK RAINEY MAKES GOOD

ALL DRINKS

FOR

ONE WEEK. NAME YOUR POISON!

"'At this yere time, it's about half through Jack Rainey's week, an' the pop'lace of Lido, in consequence, is plumb happy an' content. They're holdin' co't at the time; the same bein' the first jestice, legal, which is dealt out in Lido.'

"'An' do you-all know,' puts in Dan Boggs, who's listnein' to Tutt, 'I'm mighty distrustful of co'ts. You go to holdin' of 'em, an' it looks like everybody gets wrought up to frenzy ontil life where them forums is held ain't safe for a second. I shall shorely deplore the day when a co't goes to openin' its game in Wolfville. It's "adios" to liberty an' peace an' safety from that time.'

"'You can go a yellow stack,' remarks Texas Thompson, who sets thar plumb loquacious an' locoed to get in a speech, 'that Boggs sizes up right about them triboonals. They're a disturbin' element in any commoonity. I knowed a town in Texas which is that peaceful it's pastoral—that's what it is, it's like a sheepfold, it's so meek an' easy—ontil one day they ups an' plays a co't an' jedge an' jury on that camp; rings in a herd of law sharps, an' a passel of rangers with Winchesters to back the deal. The town's that fretted tharat it gets full of nose-paint to the brim, an' then hops into the street for gen'ral practice with its guns. In the mornin' the round-up shows two dead an' five wounded, an' all for openin' co't on an outfit which is too frail to stand the strain of so much jestice onexpected.'

"'As I'm engaged in remarkin',' says Tutt, after Boggs an' Texas is redooced to quiet ag'in—Tutt bein' married most likely is used to interruptions, an' is shore patient that a-way—'as I states, they're holdin' co't, an' this day they emancipates from prison a party named Caribou Sam. They tries to prove this Caribou Sam is a hoss-thief, but couldn't fill on the draw, an' so Caribou works free of 'em an' is what they calls "'quitted."

"'As soon as ever the marshal takes the hobbles off this Caribou Sam—he's been held a captif off some'ers an' is packed into Lido onder gyard to be tried a lot—this yere malefactor comes bulgin' into the Sunflower an' declar's for fire-water. The barkeep deals to him, an' Caribou Sam is assuaged.

"'When he goes to pay, a gent who's standin' near shoves back his dust, an' says: "This is Jack Rainey's week—it's the great anny-ooal festival of Jack Rainey, an' your money's no good."

"'"But I aims to drink some more *poco tiempo*," says this Caribou Sam, who is new to Lido, an' never yet hears of Jack Rainey an' his little game, "an' before I permits a gent to subsidize my thirst, an' go stackin'in for my base appetites, you can gamble I want to meet him an' make his acquaintance. Where is this yere sport Jack Rainey, an' whatever is he doin' this on?"

"'The party who shoves Caribou's *dinero* off the bar, tells him he can't pay, an' explains the play, an' exhorts him to drink free an' frequent an' keep his chips in his war-bags.

""As I tells you," says this party to Caribou, "my friend Jack Rainey has treed the camp, an' no money goes yere but his till his further commands is known. Fill your hide, but don't flourish no funds, or go enlargin' on any weakness you has for buyin' your own licker. As for seein' Jack Rainey, it's plumb impossible. He's got too full to visit folks or be visited by 'em; but he's upsta'rs on some blankets, an' if his reason is restored by tomorry, you sends up your kyard an' pays him your regyards—pendin' of which social function, take another drink. Barkeep, pump another dose into this stranger, an' charge the same to Jack."

""This yere sounds good," says Caribou Sam, "but it don't win over me. Ontil I sees this person Rainey, I shall shorely decline all bottles which is presented in his name. I've had a close call about a bronco I stole to-day, an' when the jury makes a verdict that they're sorry to say the evidence ain't enough to convict, the jedge warns me to be a heap careful of the company I maintains. He exhorts me to live down my past, or failin' which he'll hang me yet. With this bluff from the bench ringin in my y'ears, I shall refoose drinks with all onknown sots, ontil I sees for myse'f they's proper characters for me to be sociable with. Tharfore, barkeep, I renoo my determination to pay for them drinks; at the same time, I orders another round. Do you turn for me or no?"

""Not none you don't," says the friend of Jack Rainey. "You can drink, but you can't pay—leastwise, you-all can't pay without gettin' all sort o' action on your money. This Rainey you're worried about is as good a gent as me, an' not at all likely to shake the standin' of a common hoss-thief by merely buyin' his nosepaint."

""Mine is shorely a difficult p'sition," says Caribou Sam. "What you imparts is scarce encouragin'. If this yere Rainey ain't no improvement onto you, I absolootely weakens on him an' turns aside from all relations of his proposin'. I'm in mighty bad report as the game stands, an' I tharfore insists ag'in on payin' for my own war medicine, as bein' a move necessary to protect my attitoodes before the public."

"'With these yere observations, Caribou Sam makes a bluff at the barkeep with a handful of money. In remonstratin', Jack Rainey's pard nacherally pulls a gun, as likewise does Caribou Sam. Thar's the customary quantity of shootin', an' while neither Caribou nor his foe gets drilled, a bullet goes through the ceilin' an' sort o' sa'nters in a careless, indifferent way into pore Jack Rainey, where he's bedded down an' snorin' up above.

"'Shore, he's dead, Rainey is,' concloodes Dave, 'an' his ontimely takin' off makes Lido quit loser for three days of licker free as air. He's a splendid, gen'rous soul, Jack Rainey is; an' as I says at the beginnin', he falls a sacrifice to his love for others, an' in tryin' at his own expense to promote the happiness an' lift them burdens of his fellowmen.'

"'This yere miscreant, Caribou,' says Texas Thompson, 'is a mighty sight too punctilious about them drinks; which thar's no doubt of it. Do they lynch him?'

"'No,' says Tutt; 'from the calibre of the gun which fires the lead that snatches Rainey from us, it is cl'ar that it's the gent who's contendin' with Caribou who does it. Still public opinion is some sour over losin' them three days, an' so Caribou goes lopin' out of Lido surreptitious that same evenin', an' don't wait none on Rainey's obsequies Caribou merely sends regrets by the barkeep of the Sunflower, reiterates the right to pay for them drinks an' Lido sees him no more.'"

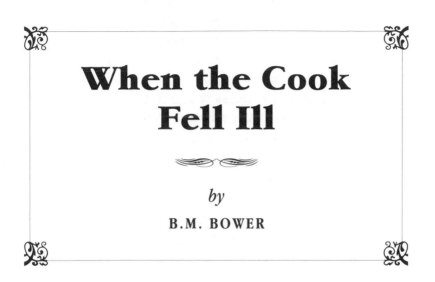

When the Cook Fell Ill

by

B.M. BOWER

I T WAS FOUR O'CLOCK, and there was consternation in the roundup camp of the Flying U; when one eats breakfast before dawn—July dawn at that—covers thirty miles of rough country before eleven o'clock dinner and as many more after, supper seems, for the time being, the most important thing in the life of a cowboy.

Men stood about in various dejected attitudes, their thumbs tucked inside their chap belts, blank helplessness writ large upon their perturbed countenances—they were the aliens, hired but to make a full crew during roundup. Long-legged fellows with spurs a-jingle hurried in and out of the cook tent, colliding often, shouting futile questions, commands and maledictions—they were the Happy Family: loyal, first and last to the Flying U, feeling a certain degree of proprietorship and a good deal of responsibility.

Happy Jack was fanning an incipient blaze in the sheet-iron stove with his hat, his face red and gloomy at the prospect of having to satisfy fifteen outdoor appetites with his amateur attempts at cooking. Behind the stove, writhing bulkily upon a hastily unrolled bed, lay Patsy, groaning most pitiably.

"What the devil's the matter with that hot water?" Cal Emmett yelled at Happy Jack from the bedside, where he was kneeling sympathetically.

Happy Jack removed his somber gaze from the licking tongue of flame which showed in the stove front. "Fire ain't going good, yet," he said in a matter-of-fact tone which contrasted sharply with Cal's excitement. "Teakettle's dry, too. I sent a man to the crick for a bucket uh water; he'll be back in a minute."

"Well, *move!* If it was you tied in a knot with cramp, yuh wouldn't take it so serene."

"Aw, gwan. I got troubles enough, cooking chuck for this here layout. I got to have some help—and lots of it. Patsy ain't got enough stuff cooked up to feed a jackrabbit. Somebody's got to mosey in here and peel the spuds."

"That's your funeral," said Cal, unfeelingly.

Chip stuck his head under the lifted tent flap. "Say, I can't find that cussed Three-H bottle," he complained. "What went with it, Cal?"

"Ask Slim; he had it last. Ain't Shorty here, yet?" Cal turned again to Patsy, whose outcries were not nice to listen to. "Stay with it, old-timer; we'll have something hot to pour down yuh in a minute."

Patsy replied, but pain made him incoherent. Cal caught the word "poison," and then "corn"; the rest of the sentence was merely a succession of groans.

The face of Cal lengthened perceptibly. He got up and went out to where the others were wrangling with Slim over the missing bottle of liniment.

"I guess the old boy's up against it good and plenty," he announced gravely. "He says he's poisoned; he says it was the corn."

"Well he had it coming to him," declared Jack Bates. "He's stuck that darned canned corn under our noses every meal since roundup started. He—"

"Oh, shut up," snarled Cal. "I guess it won't be so funny if he cashes in on the strength of it. I've known two or three fellows that was laid out cold with tin-can poison. It's sure fierce."

The Happy Family shifted uneasily before the impending tragedy, and their faces paled a little; for nearly every man of the range dreads ptomaine poisoning more than the bite of a rattler. One can kill a rattler, and one is always warned of its presence; but one never can tell what dire suffering may lurk beneath the gay labels of canned goods. But since one must eat, and since canned vegetables are far and away better than no vegetables at all, the Happy Family ate and took their chance—only they did not eat canned corn, and they had discussed the matter profanely and often with Patsy.

Patsy was a slave of precedent. Many seasons had he cooked beneath a roundup tent, and never had he stocked the mess wagon for a long trip and left canned corn off the list. It was good to his palate and it was easy to prepare, and no argument could wean him from imperturbably opening can after can, eating plentifully of it himself and throwing the rest to feed the gophers.

"Ain't there anything to give him?" asked Jack, relenting. "That Three-H would fix him up all right—"

"Dig it up, then," snapped Cal. "There's sure something got to be done, or we'll have a dead cook on our hands."

"Not even a drop uh whisky in camp!" mourned Weary. "Slim, you ought to be killed for getting away with that liniment."

Slim was too downhearted to resent the tone. "By golly, I can't think what I done with it after I used it on Banjo. Seems like I stood it on that rock—"

"Oh, hell!" snorted Cal. "That's forty miles back."

"Say, it's sure a fright!" sympathized Jack Bates as a muffled shriek came through the cloth wall of the tent. "What's good for tin-caneetis, I wonder?"

"A rattling good doctor," retorted Chip, throwing things recklessly about, still searching. "There goes the damn butter—pick it up, Cal."

"If Old Dock was sober, he could do something," suggested Weary. "I guess I'd better go after him; what do yuh think?"

"He could send out some stuff—if he was sober enough; he's sure wise on medicine."

Weary made him a cigarette. "Well, it's me for Dry Lake," he said, crisply. "I reckon Patsy can hang on till I get back; can poison doesn't do the business inside several hours, and he hasn't been sick long. He was all right when Happy Jack hit camp about two o'clock. I'll be back by dark—I'll ride Glory." He swung up on the nearest horse, which happened to be Chip's, and raced out to the saddle bunch a quarter of a mile away. The Happy Family watched him go and called after him, urging him unnecessarily to speed.

Weary did not waste time having the bunch corralled but rode in among the horses, his rope down and ready for business. Glory stared curiously, tossed his crimpled, silver mane, dodged a second too late and found himself caught.

It was unusual, this interruption just when he was busy cropping sweet grasses and taking his ease, but he supposed there was some good reason for it; at any rate he submitted quietly to being saddled and merely nipped Weary's shoulder once and struck out twice with an ivory-white, daintily rounded hoof—and Weary was grateful for the docile mood he showed.

He mounted hurriedly without a word of praise or condemnation, and his silence was to Glory more unusual than being roped and saddled on the range. He seemed to understand that the stress was great, and fairly bolted up the long, western slope of the creek bottom straight toward the slant of the sun.

For two miles he kept the pace unbroken, though the way was not of the smoothest and there was no trail to follow. Straight away to the west, with fifteen miles of hills and coulees between, lay Dry Lake; and in Dry Lake lived the one man in the country who might save Patsy.

"Old Dock" was a landmark among old-timers. The oldest pioneer found Dock before him among the Indians and buffalo that ran riot over the wind-brushed prairie where now the nation's beef feeds quietly. Why he was there no man could tell; he was a fresh-faced young Frenchman with much knowledge of medicine and many theories, and a reticence un-French. From the Indians he learned to use strange herbs that healed almost magically the ills of man; from the rough outcroppings of civilization he learned to swallow vile whiskey in great gulps, and to thirst always for more.

So he grew old while the West was yet young, until Dry Lake, which grew up around him, could not remember him as any but a white-bearded, stooped shuffling old man who spoke a queer jargon and was always just getting drunk or sober. When he was sober his medicines never failed to cure; when he was drunk he could not be induced to prescribe, so that men trusted his wisdom at all times and tolerated his infirmities, and looked upon him with amused proprietorship.

When Weary galloped up the trail which, because a few habitations are strewn with fine contempt of regularity upon either side, is called by courtesy a street, his eyes sought impatiently for the familiar, patriarchal figure of Old Dock. He felt that minutes were worth much and that if he would save Patsy he must cut out all superfluities, so he resolutely declined to remember that cold, foamy beer refreshes one amazingly after a long, hot ride in the dust and the wind.

Upon the porch of Rusty Brown's place men were gathered, and it was evident even at a distance that they were mightily amused. Weary headed for the spot and stopped beside the hitching pole. Old Dock stood in the center of the group and his bent old figure was trembling with rage. With both hands he waved aloft his coat, on which was plastered a sheet of "tangle-foot" flypaper.

"Das wass de mean treeck!" he was shouting. "I don'd do de harm wis no mans. I tend mine business, I buy me mine clothes. De mans wass do dees treeck, he buy me new clothes—you bet you! Dass wass de mean—"

"Say, Dock," broke in Weary, towering over him, "you dig up some dope for tin-can poison, and do it quick. Patsy's took bad."

Old Dock looked up at him and shook his shaggy, white beard. "Das wass de mean treeck," he repeated, waving the coat at Weary. "You see dass? Mine coat, she ruint; dass was new coat!"

"All right—I'll take your word for it, Dock. Tell me what's good for tin—"

"Aw, I knows you fellers. You t'ink Ole Dock, she Dock, she don'd know nothings! You t'ink—"

Weary sighed and turned to the crowd. "Which end of a jag is this?" he wanted to know. "I've got to get some uh that dope-wisdom out uh him, somehow. Patsy's a goner, sure, if I don't connect with some medicine."

The men crowded close and asked questions which Weary felt bound to answer; everyone knew Patsy, who was almost as much a part of Dry Lake scenery as was Old Dock, and it was gratifying to a Flying U man to see the sympathy in their faces. But Patsy needed something more potent than sympathy, and the minutes were passing.

Old Dock still discoursed whimperingly upon the subject of his ruined coat and the meanness of mankind, and there was no weaning his interest for a moment, try as Weary would. And fifteen miles away in a picturesque creek bottom a man lay dying in great pain for want of one little part of the wisdom stored uselessly away in the brain of this drunken, doddering old man.

Weary's gloved hand dropped in despair from Old Dock's bent shoulder. "Damn a drunkard!" he said bitterly, and got into the saddle. "Rusty, I'll want to borrow that calico cayuse uh yours. Have him saddled up right away, will yuh? I'll be back in a little bit."

He jerked his hat down to his eyebrows and struck Glory with the quirt; but the trail he took was strange to Glory and he felt impelled to stop and argue—as only Glory could argue—with his master. Minutes passed tumultuously, with nothing accomplished save some weird hoofprints in the sod. Eventually, however, Glory gave over trying to stand upon his head and his hind feet at one and the same instant, and permitted himself to be guided toward a certain tiny, low-eaved cabin in a meadow just over the hill from the town.

Weary was not by nature given to burglary, but he wrenched open the door of the cabin and went in, with not a whisper of conscience to say him nay. It was close and ill-smelling and very dirty inside, but after the first whiff Weary did not notice it. He went over and stopped before a little, old-fashioned chest; it was padlocked, so he left that as a last resort and searched elsewhere for what he wanted—medicine. Under the bed he found a flat, black case, such as old-fashioned doctors carried. He drew it out and examined it critically. This, also, was locked, but he shook it tentatively and heard the faintest possible jingle inside.

"Bottles," he said briefly, and grinned satisfaction. Something brushed against his hat and he looked up into a very dusty bunch of herbs. "You too," he told them, breaking the string with one yank. "For all I know, yuh might stand ace-high in this game. Lord! if I could trade brains with the old devil, just for tonight!"

He took a last look around, decided that he had found all he wanted, and went out and pulled the door shut. Then he tied the black medicine case to the saddle in a way that would give it the least jar, stuffed the bunch of dried herbs into his pocket and mounted for the homeward race. As he did so the sun threw a red beam into his eyes as though reminding him of the passing hours, and ducked behind the ridge which bounds Lonesome Prairie on the east.

The afterglow filled sky and earth with a soft, departing radiance when he stopped again in front of the saloon. Old Dock was still gesticulating wildly, and the sheet of flypaper still clung to the back of his coat. The crowd had thinned somewhat and displayed less interest; otherwise the situation had not changed, except that a pinto pony stood meekly, with head drooping, at the hitching pole.

"There's your horse," Rusty Brown called to Weary. "Yours played out?"

"Not on your life," Weary denied proudly. "When yuh see Glory played out, you'll see him with four feet in the air."

"I seen him that way half an hour ago, all right," bantered Bert Rogers.

Weary passed over the joke. "Mamma! Has it been that long?" he cried uneasily. "I've got to be moving some. Here, Dock, you put on that coat—and never mind the label; it's got to go—and so have you."

"Aw, he's no good to yuh, Weary," they protested. "He's too drunk to tell chloroform from dried apricots."

"That'll be all right," Weary assured them confidently. "I guess he'll be some sober by the time we hit camp. I went and dug up his dope-box, so he can get right to work when he arrives. Send him out here."

"Say, he can't never top off Powderface, Weary. I thought yuh was going to ride him yourself. It's plumb wicked to put that old centurion on him. He wouldn't be able to stay with him a mile."

"That's a heap farther than he could get with Glory," said Weary, unmoved. "Yuh don't seem to realize that Patsy's just next thing to a dead man, and Dock has got the name of what'll cure him sloshing around amongst all that whiskey in his head. I can't wait for him to sober up—I'm just plumb obliged to take him along, jag and all. Come on, Dock; this is a lovely evening for a ride."

Dock objected emphatically with head, arms, legs and much mixed dialect. But Weary climbed down and, with the help of Bert Rogers, carried him bodily and lifted him into the saddle. When the pinto began to offer some objections, strong hands seized his bridle and held him angrily submissive.

"He'll tumble off, sure as yuh live," predicted Bert; but Weary never did things by halves; he shook his head and untied his coiled rope.

"By the Lord! I hate to see a man ride into town and pack off the only heirloom we got," complained Rusty Brown. "Dock's been handed down from generation to Genesis, and there ain't hardly a scratch on him. If yuh don't bring him back in good order, Weary Davidson, there'll be things doing."

Weary looked up from taking the last half-hitch around the saddle horn. "Yuh needn't worry," he said. "This medical monstrosity is more valuable to me than he is to you, right now. I'll handle him careful."

"Das wass de mean treeck!" cried Dock, for all the world like a parrot.

"It sure is, old boy," assented Weary cheerfully, and tied the pinto's bridle reins into a hard knot at the end. With the reins in his hand he mounted Glory. "Your pinto'll lead, won't he?" he asked Rusty then. It was like Weary to take a thing for granted first, and ask questions about it afterward.

"Maybe he will—he never did, so far," grinned Rusty. "It's plumb insulting to a self-respecting cow pony to make a packhorse out uh him. I wouldn't be none surprised if yuh heard his views on the subject before yuh git there."

"It's an honor to pack heirlooms," retorted Weary. "So long, boys."

Old Dock made a last, futile effort to free himself and then settled down in the saddle and eyed the world sullenly from under frost-white eyebrows heavy as a military mustache. He did not at that time look particularly patriarchal; more nearly he resembled a humbled, entrapped Santa Claus.

They started off quite tamely. The pinto leaned far back upon the bridle reins and trotted with stiff, reluctant legs that did not promise speed; but still he went, and Weary drew a relieved breath.

His arm was like to ache frightfully before they covered a quarter of the fifteen miles, but he did not mind that much; besides, he guessed shrewdly that the pinto would travel better once they were well out of town.

The soft, warm dusk of a July evening crept over the land and a few stars winked at them facetiously. Over by the reedy creek, frogs *cr-ek-ek-ekked* in a tuneless medley and nighthawks flapped silently through the still air, swooping suddenly with a queer, *whooing* rush like wind blowing through a cavern. Familiar sounds they were to Weary—so familiar that he scarce heard them; though he would have felt a vague, uneasy sense of something lost had they stilled unexpectedly. Out in the lane which led to the open range-land between wide reaches of rank blue-joint meadows, a new sound met them—the faint, insistent humming of millions of mosquitoes. Weary dug Glory with his spurs and came near having his arm jerked from its socket before he could pull him in again. He swore a little and swung round in the saddle.

"Can't yuh dig a little speed into that cayuse with your heels, Dock?" he cried to the resentful heirloom. "We're going to be naturally chewed up if we don't fan the breeze along here."

"Ah don'd care—das wass de mean treeck!" growled Dock into his beard.

Weary opened his mouth, came near swallowing a dozen mosquitoes alive, and closed it again. What would it profit him to argue with a drunken man? He slowed till the pinto, still moving with stiff, reluctant knees, came alongside, and struck him sharply with his quirt; the pinto sidled and Dock lurched over as far as Weary's rope would permit.

"Come along, then!" admonished Weary, under his breath.

The pinto snorted and ran backward until Weary wished he had been content with the pace of a snail. Then the mosquitoes swooped down upon them in a cloud and Glory struck out, fighting and kicking viciously. Presently Weary found himself with part of the pinto's bridle rein in his hand, and the memory of a pale object disappearing into the darkness ahead.

For the time being he was wholly occupied with his own horse; but when Glory was minded to go straight ahead instead of in a circle, he gave thought to his mission and thanked the Lord that Dock was headed in the right direction. He gave chase joyfully; for every mile covered in that fleet fashion meant an added chance for Patsy's life. Even the mosquitoes found themselves hopelessly out of the race and beat up harmlessly in the rear. So he galloped steadily upon the homeward trail; and a new discomfort forced itself upon his consciousness—the discomfort of swift riding while a sharp-cornered medicine-case of generous proportions thumped regularly against his leg. At first he did not mind it so much, but after ten minutes of riding so, the thing grew monotonously painful and disquieting to the nerves.

Five miles from the town he sighted the pinto; it was just disappearing up a coulee which led nowhere—much less to camp. Weary's self-congratulatory mood changed to impatience; he followed after. Two miles, and he reached the unclimbable head of the coulee—and no pinto. He pulled up and gazed incredulously at the blank, sandstone walls; searched long for some hidden pathway to the top and gave it up.

He rode back slowly under the stars, a much disheartened Weary. He thought of Patsy's agony and gritted his teeth at his own impotence. After a while he thought of Old Dock lashed to the pinto's saddle, and his conscience awoke and badgered him unmercifully for the thing he had done and the risk he had taken with one man's life that he might save the life of another.

Down near the mouth of the coulee he came upon a cattle trail winding up toward the stars. For the lack of a better clue he turned into it and urged Glory faster than was wise if he would save the strength of his horse; but Glory was game as long as he could stand, and took the hill at a lope with never a protest against the pace.

Up on the top the prairie stretched mysteriously away to the skyline with no sound to mar the broody silence, and with never a movement to disturb the deep sleep of the grassland. All day had the hills been buffeted by a sweeping west wind; but the breeze had dropped with the sun, as though tired with roistering, and slept without so much as a dream-puff to shake the dew from the grasses.

Weary stopped to wind his horse and to listen, but not a hoof-beat came to guide him in his search. He leaned and shifted the medicine case a bit to ease his bruised leg, and wished he might unlock the healing mysteries and the magic stored within. It seemed to him a cruel world and unjust that knowledge must be gleaned slowly, laboriously, while men died miserably for want of it. Worse, that men who had gleaned should be permitted to smother such precious knowledge in the stupefying fumes of whiskey.

If he could only have appropriated Dock's brain along with his medicines, he might have been in camp by now, ministering to Patsy before it was too late to do anything. Without a doubt the boys were scanning anxiously the ridge, confident that he would not fail them though impatient for his coming. And here he sat helplessly upon a hilltop under the stars, many miles from camp, with much medicine just under his knee and a pocket crammed with an unknown, healing herb, as useless after all his effort as he had been in camp when they could not find the Three-H liniment.

Glory turned his head and regarded him gravely out of eyes near human in their questioning, and Weary laid caressing hand upon his silvery mane, grateful for the sense of companionship which it gave.

"You're sure a wise little nag," he said wistfully, and his voice sounded strange in the great silence. "Maybe you can find 'em—and if you can, I'll sure be grateful; you can paw the stars out uh high heaven and I won't take my quirt off my saddle horn; hope I may die if I do!"

Glory stamped one white hoof and pointed both ears straight forward, threw up his head and whinnied a shrill question into the night. Weary hopefully urged him with his knees. Glory challenged once again and struck out eagerly, galloping lightly in spite of the miles he had covered. Far back on the benchland came faint answer to his call, and Weary laughed from sheer relief. By the stars the night was yet young, and he grew hopeful—almost complacent.

Glory planted both forefeet deep in the prairie sod and skidded on the brink of a deep cut-bank. It was a close shave, such as comes often to those who ride the range by night. Weary looked down into blackness and then across into gloom. The place was too deep and sheer to ride into, and too wide to jump; clearly, they must go around it.

Going around a gully is not always the simple thing it sounds, especially when one is not sure as to the direction it takes. To find the head under such conditions requires time.

Weary thought he knew the place and turned north secure in the belief that the gully ran south into the coulee he had that evening fruitlessly explored. As a matter of fact it opened into a coulee north of them, and in that direction it grew always deeper and more impassable even by daylight.

On a dark night, with only the stars to guide one and to accentuate the darkness, such a discovery brings with it confusion of locality. Weary drew up when he could go no farther without plunging headlong into blackness, and mentally sketched a map of that particular portion of the globe and tried to find in it a place where the gulch might consistently lie. After a minute he gave over the attempt and admitted to himself that, according to his mental map, it could not consistently lie anywhere at all. Even Glory seemed to have lost interest in the quest and stood listlessly with his head down. His attitude irritated Weary very much.

"Yuh damn', taffy-colored cayuse!" he said fretfully. "This is as much your funeral as mine—seeing yuh started out all so brisk to find that pinto. Do yuh suppose yuh could find a horse if he was staked ten feet in front of your nose? Chances are, yuh couldn't. I reckon you'd have trouble finding your way around the little pasture at the ranch—unless the sun shone real bright and yuh had somebody to lead yuh!"

This was manifestly unjust and it was not like Weary; but this night's mission was getting on his nerves. He leaned and shifted the medicine case again, and felt ruefully of his bruised leg. That also was getting upon his nerves.

"Oh, Mamma!" he muttered disgustedly. "This is sure a sarcastic layout; dope enough here to cure all the sickness in Montana—if a fellow knew enough to use it—battering a hole in my leg you could throw a yearling calf into, and me wandering wild over the hills like a locoed sheepherder! Glory, you get a move on yuh, you knock-kneed, buzzard-headed—" He subsided into incoherent grumbling and rode back whence he came, up the gully's brim.

When the night was far gone and the slant of the Great Dipper told him that day-dawn was near, he heard a horse nicker wistfully, away to the right. Wheeling sharply, his spurs raking the roughened sides of Glory, he rode recklessly toward the sound, not daring to hope that it might be the pinto and yet holding his mind back from despair.

When he was near the place—so near that he could see a dim, formless shape outlined against the skyline—Glory stumbled over a sunken rock and fell heavily upon his knees. When he picked himself up he hobbled and Weary cursed him unpityingly.

When, limping painfully, Glory came up with the object, the heart of Weary rose up and stuck in his throat; for the object was a pinto horse and above it bulked the squat figure of an irate old man.

"Hello, Dock," greeted Weary. "How do yuh stack up?"

"Mon Dieu, Weary Davitson, I feex yous plandy. What for do you dees t'ing? I not do de harrm wis you. I not got de mooney

wort' all dees troubles what you makes. Dees horse, she lak for keel me also. She buck, en keeck, en roon—*mon Dieu,* I not like dees t'ing."

"Sober, by thunder!" ejaculated Weary in an ecstatic half-whisper. "Dock, you've got a chance to make a record for yourself tonight—if we ain't too late," he added bodefully. "Do yuh know where we're headed for?"

"I t'ink for de devil," retorted Old Dock peevishly.

"No sir, we aren't. We're going straight to camp, and you're going to save old Patsy—you like Patsy, you know; many's the time you've tanked up together and then fell on each other's necks and wept because the good old times won't come again. He got poisoned on canned corn; the Lord send he ain't too dead for you to cure him. Come on—we better hit the breeze. We've lost a heap uh time."

"I not like dees rope; she not comforte. I have ride de bad horse when you wass in cradle."

Weary got down and went over to him. "All right, I'll unwind yuh. When we started yuh know, yuh couldn't uh rode a rocking chair. I was plumb obliged to tie yuh on. Think we'll be in time to help Patsy? He was taken sick about four o'clock."

Old Dock waited till he was untied and the remnant of bridle rein was placed in his hand, before he answered ironically: "I not do de mageec, *mon cher* Weary. I mos' have de medicine or I can do nottings, I not wave de fingaire an' say de vord."

"That's all right—I've got the whole works. I broke into your shack and made a clean haul uh dope. And I want to tell yuh that for a doctor you've got blame poor ventilation to your house. But I found the medicine."

"Mon Dieu!" was the astonished comment, and after that they rode in silence and such haste as Glory's lameness would permit.

The first beams of the sun were touching redly the hilltops and the birds were singing from swaying weeds when they rode down the last slope into the valley where camped the Flying U.

The nighthawk had driven the horses into the rope-corral and men were inside watching, with spread loop, for a chance to throw. Happy Jack, with the cook's apron tied tightly around his lank middle stood despondently in the doorway of the mess tent and said no word as they approached. In his silence—in his very presence there—Weary read disaster.

"I guess we're too late," he told Dock, in hushed tones; for the minute he hated the white-bearded old man whose drunkenness had cost the Flying U so dear. He slipped wearily from the saddle and let the reins drop to the ground. Happy Jack still eyed them silently.

"Well?" asked Weary, when his nerves would bear no more.

"When I git sick," said Happy Jack, his voice heavy with reproach, "I'll send *you* for help—if I want to die."

"Is he dead?" questioned Weary, in hopeless fashion.

"Well," said Happy Jack deliberately, "no, he ain't dead yet—but it's no thanks to *you*. Was it poker or billiards? and who won?"

Weary looked at him dully a moment before he comprehended. He had not had any supper or any sleep, and he had ridden many miles in the long hours he had been away. He walked, with a pronounced limp on the leg which had been next the medicine case, to where Dock stood leaning shakily against the pinto.

"Maybe we're in time, after all," he said slowly. "Here's some kind uh dried stuff I got off the ceiling; I thought maybe yuh might need it—you're great on Indian weeds." He pulled a crumpled, faintly aromatic bundle of herbs from his pocket.

Dock took it and sniffed disgustedly, and dropped the herbs contemptuously to the ground. "Dat not wort' notting—she what you call—de—cat*neep.*" He smiled sourly.

Weary cast a furtive glance at Happy Jack, and hoped he had not overheard. Catnip! Still, how could he be expected to know what the blamed stuff was? He untied the black medicine case and brought it and put it at the feet of Old Dock. "Well, here's the joker, anyhow," he said. "It like to wore a hole clear through my leg, but I was careful and I don't believe any uh the bottles are busted."

Dock looked at it and sat heavily down upon a box. He looked at the case queerly, then lifted his shaggy head to gaze up at Weary. And behind the bleared gravity of his eyes was something very like a twinkle. "Dis, she not cure seek mans, neider. She—" He pressed a tiny spring which Weary had not discovered and laid the case open upon the ground. "You see?" he said plaintively. "She not good for Patsy—she tree dossen can-openaire."

Weary stared blankly. Happy Jack came up, looked and doubled convulsively. Can openers! Three dozen of them. Old Dock was explaining in his best English, and he was courteously refraining from the faintest smile.

"Dey de new, bettaire kind. I send for dem, I t'ink maybe I sell. I put her in de grip—so—I carry dem all togedder. My mediceen, she in de beeg ches'."

Weary had sat down and his head was dropped dejectedly into his hands. He had bungled the whole thing, after all. "Well," he said apathetically, "the chest was locked; I never opened it."

Old Dock nodded his head gravely. "She lock," he assented, gently. "She mooch mediceen—she wort' mooch mooney. De key, she in mine pocket—"

"Oh, I don't give a damn where the key is—now," flared Weary. "I guess Patsy'll have to cash in; that's all."

"Aw, gwan!" cried Happy Jack. "A sheepman come along just after you left, and he had a quart uh whiskey. We begged it off him and give Patsy a good bit jolt. That eased him up some, and we give him another—and he got to hollerin' so loud for more uh the same, so we just set the bottle in easy reach and let him alone. He's in there now, drunk as a biled owl—the lazy old devil. I had to get supper and breakfast too—and looks like I'd have to cook dinner. Poison—hell! I betche he never had nothing but a plain old belly-ache!"

Weary got up and went to the mess tent, lifted the flap and looked in upon Patsy lying on the flat of his back, snoring comfortably. He regarded him silently a moment, then looked over his shoulder to where Old Dock huddled over the three dozen can openers.

"Oh, Mamma!" he whispered, and poured himself a cup of coffee.

The Punchers Tell a Few

by

ROSS SANTEE

IT WAS LATE THAT EVENIN' when we rode into the ranch. Us kids was soakin' wet an' nearly starved, but we set there on our horses a-starin' at the place until the tall puncher spoke.

"You boys turn loose," he says, "an' come on in an' eat. You can put your ponies in that little trap an' you'd better put your saddles in the shed, for it's pretty wet out here."

He showed us where to put our stuff, an' as we follered him inside I never missed a thing he wore. From his high-heeled boots an' overalls to that high-crowned Stetson hat. The overalls I'd always seen an' wore had bibs an' shoulder-straps. But these of his come only to his waist. He wore them turned up at the bottom, an' they had narrow stove-pipe legs. It didn't surprise me none to see the big hat an' high-heeled boots, for I'd always figgered that was what a cowboy wore. But I made up my mind first chance I got I'd ditch the overalls I had an' get a pair like his.

The outfit had finished supper, an' the room was full of smoke. At the end of the long table where they eat four cowboys an' the cook was playin' cards. An' over in one corner of the room some more was shootin' dice. There must have been fifteen punchers in the place. Some was settin' on their heels around the room just smokin' cigarettes. One puncher who didn't look to be much older than me was workin' on a saddle. Another one alongside of him was braidin' a rawhide rope. I figered he must own the place, for his hair was white as snow. Some of them nodded to us when we come in, but most of them didn't speak.

It was the tall black-headed puncher that cooked somethin' for us to eat. I follered him into the kitchen. For everything seemed strange to me, an' there was somethin' friendly about this tall black-headed guy although he didn't talk. There was plenty of frijole beans already cooked. But he made more coffee an' fried steak an' cooked more bread for us. It was the first time I'd ever seen anyone 'cept a woman cook. But he made biscuits an' had them in the stove as quick as mother could.

As soon as he got this stuff all on he squatted on his heels an' rolled another cigarette. At intervals he looked inside to see how the bread was comin' on, or mebbe he'd chunk the fire with dried cow-chips from a gunny sack. But he never said a word. There was a thousand questions on my mind that shore was eatin' me. An' I finally up an' asked him if the old white-headed man was the owner of the ranch. He shook his head an' took a big pull at his cigarette. "Dad's just a hand," he says.

Charlie's uncle John had told me the foreman's name was Steve, so I asked him which one of them was him. He took another long pull on his cigarette. "I am," was all he says. He was friendly enough all right in spite of the fact that he was mighty sparin' with his talk. I wanted to go to work an' I figgered that now was as good a time as any to hit him for a job.

"If you'd have come a few days earlier," he says, "I might have put you on."

"I want to work," I says, "an' I'm willin' to do most anything."

"You're welcome to stay an' rest your pony up," he says, "but the outfit's full-handed now."

When I asked him about the outfits further west he said he didn't know. But he thought that work was pretty scarce at them, unless a man was a real cowhand. I didn't know it at the time, but he was tryin' to spare my feelin's with his talk. For he could have told me easy enough that there wasn't nothin' around a cow outfit that I was fit to do. At other outfits where I stopped they always told me the same old thing—if I'd have dropped in just a few days earlier they might have put me on. But instead of me a-realizin' that I knew nothin' of punchin' cows, I thought the reason I was jinxed was that every time I rode up to a ranch I was always a few days late.

I helped Steve with the dishes after Charlie an' me had eat. An' then we all went into the room where the other punchers was. Steve parked himself on his heels again. An' we set down alongside of him. For there was somethin' friendly about him—if he didn't have nothin' to say. An' the talk of the other punchers was all so strange to me. I couldn't foller them. It seems a puncher named Bill Wilson had broke the dice game up. He was a runty feller with curly hair an' one missin' tooth in front. An' instead of the overalls that most of the punchers wore he had on a pair of khaki pants that was tucked inside his boots. An' he wore the biggest hat an' pair of spurs I'd ever seen before. Dad had quit braidin' on his rope an' was settin' in the poker game. For they had broke the cook, it seems. He was the only man inside the room except us kids that wasn't wearin' boots an' spurs. An' the flour sack he used for an apron was still tied around his waist.

The room was a long, low-roofed affair with pictures tacked up around the walls. Most of them was from the Police Gazette, an' there was lots of naked women. But one picture was a page from "Life." It showed a bunch of city fellers shootin' at a cowboy's feet, an' underneath it says, "A Tenderfoot in New York." Next to it was a drawin' by Charlie Russell of a pitchin' horse, a calendar from a saddle house, an' then more naked women. Some six-shooters with cartridge-belts, an' some yeller slickers hung from nails around the wall. Along with odds an' ends of rope, some wore-out pants, a pair of leather chaps, a coat or two, an' some sacks of dirty clothes. In one corner of the room was piled some bedrolls, all tied an' corded up. An' in another corner three 30-30's stood.

A red-haired puncher told some yarn about the last time he'd been to town. I couldn't foller all of it. But it seems he met some pretty girl. An' the punchers all started laughin when he told them how he left town. An' then Bill Wilson told us about a trip he'd made to Chicago once, when he went up there with a load of stock.

"After I turned the cattle over," he says, "I had a couple of hours yet before my train pulled out. So I thought I'd see the town. I mounted the first street-car that come by, for I'd never rode one of them before. It was about five in the evenin' when I mounted her, an' everythin' went fine at first. For I was seein' lots of things that was new to me. But people kept gettin' on the car till we was packed just like sardines. I didn't mind at first for I was sittin' by a window, a-takin' in the sights. I never saw so many people in my whole life. For they swarmed out of every canyon that we passed just like a bunch of ants. I thought at first there was a fire some place. But when I asked the feller sittin' next to me he laughs an' says they was comin' home from work. So I didn't talk to him no more.

"We rode for an hour, mebbe. An' I begun to figger if I was goin' to ketch my train I'd better be gettin' off. But there wasn't no chance of that. For the car was still jam full. I didn't know what to do, so I set there for mebbe thirty minutes more. When finally this feller settin' next to me, he up an' fights his way right through the crowd an' yells he's gettin' off. I took my cue from him an' stayed right at that hombre's heels. For he went right through them people like an old steer through the brush. I lost two buttons off my coat but I made it off the car.

"I didn't have no idea where the depot was so I finally asked a cop. An' he told me it was only two blocks off an' pointed the thing right out to me. I figgered I was jake. For I'd seen lots of the city an' had a good street-car ride. But when I got into the depot they told me it wasn't the place. I never had no idea there was more than one depot in the town. An' I only had twenty minutes to ketch my train. I didn't know what to do. For I knowed I'd never find the other depot now. But the feller in the ticket place tells me to take a cab. The feller that drove the cab was nothin' but a kid, but he shore did know the town. I've been there once since then. But that one trip cured me of tryin' to run around. For next time as soon as I turned the cattle over I rolled my tail for home."

The red-haired puncher finally looked at me an' Charlie as if he'd just discovered us an' asked where we was from.

"East Texas," says Charlie.

"That so?" the redhead says. "Did they dip you boys when you crossed the line from Texas into New Mexico?"

"No," Charlie says; an' then I spoke up an' asked him what they should dip us for.

"Ticks," the redhead says. "You boys may not know it, but you have broke the law. For it says that all people comin' from Texas to New Mexico must be dipped 'long with their stock."

"Uncle John never told us anything like that an' I guess he'd know," says Charlie.

"Your uncle John knows well enough," Red says, "an' if they find out he sent you boys acrost the line without dippin' you, they can send your uncle up. Of course, I wouldn't say a word myself. For I wouldn't make trouble for no man. But if the law was to find out that we took you in, they could make it hard on us. Of course, I'm just a-workin' here myself an' I guess that's up to Steve."

Charlie an' I both looked at Steve. I had some doubts of Red. But anythin' Steve said went down with me for he was the foreman of the ranch. Steve pulled a long time at his cigarette an' finally he says. "That's right; I'd hate to make trouble for his uncle John. An' I'd hate to see these boys go off to jail. But if we dip them here at the ranch we can get around the law."

"We ain't got ticks," I says.

"How do you know?" says Red. "For all you care, the whole out-fit might get lousy as a pet coon with them, just because of you two kids."

Finally I says, "All right." For I figgered if it had to be done we might as well get it over with. But Steve says as long as we've put it off this long we could wait till tomorrow mornin'.

From ticks they switched the conversation to skunks. "I ain't afraid of them," I says, "for I've trapped lots of skunks at home."

"Kid," says Bill Wilson, speakin' up, "you ain't never seen no skunks like the kind they got out here. Of course, these skunks out here smells pretty much the same as the ones you're speakin' of, but these out here goes mad."

I remembered of hearin' of hydrophobia skunks some place an' I sort of looked at Steve.

He took a long pull on his cigarette. "I reckon it's so," he says. "But there ain't as many of them around the ranch right now as there is at other times. It must be goin' on six months now since that last man here was bit."

"Funny thing," says Bill Wilson. "I never could figger how that skunk ever got inside the house, unless he come in at the window, an' this feller that he bit had only been here just a day. He was sleepin' in the other room right next to here, where you kids will sleep tonight. Me an' Red was sleepin' in this room, an' first thing we knowed that anythin' was wrong we heard him yellin'; an' here he come a-tearin' right through this room an' right on out the door, a-slobberin' at the mouth. We was shore scairt all right."

"I'll say we was," says Red.

"What did you do?" we says.

"Well, there wasn't much that we could do till it got daylight. But me an' Red set up the rest of the night with our guns right in our hands, for we was afraid he might come back at any time an' bite either me or Red, or mebbe bite the both of us. But as soon as it got light we saddled up an' cut for sign. We finally jumped him out, but we couldn't any more ketch him on a horse than we could fly. But finally, after we run him nearly half a day, we managed to get close enough that Red could get a shot at him."

We looked at Red. "What did you shoot him for?" we says.

Red shook his head. "I never hated to kill a man as much as I did him. But we couldn't have him runnin' loose that way, for he might bite someone."

I don't know how Charlie felt. But things was comin' too fast for me. At first I figgered it was a lie an' then again I didn't know.

After Bill Wilson an' Red had finished their yarn they went outside the house. But in a little while they come on back an' went to playin' cards. There was no one else playin' now 'cept them two. An' no one paid any hed to them till they started talkin' loud. But as soon as Bill started cussin' him Red made a grab for his gun. An' with that Bill dropped his cards an' made a run towards us kids.

That was enough for Charlie an' me, for as soon as we saw Red's gun we made a break for the door. As we hit the door we heard a shot, but we never did look back. An' just as we heard them shoot again, we hit the rope they had stretched outside an' we both went flat to the ground. It was only a second till we was up again an' on our way. But in that one second Charlie had run clear off from me. They was still shootin' from the door, so finally I laid down an' flattened out as flat as I could get. An' as I laid there wonderin' how many had been killed I heard some puncher laugh. At first I didn't get it an' I wondered what he meant. For shootin' a man in a card game was no laughin' thing to me.

An' then I heard another puncher say, "Didn't that skinny one run!" Then another puncher spoke. "That little one never throwed off none that I could see." An' then the whole bunch laughed.

When I finally got it through my head that the thing was all a joke I come on back an' tried to laugh it off. But there's no denyin' I was scairt, an' they had to hunt Charlie up.

The whole bunch set around an' laughed when we got inside the house. Finally Steve said it must be gettin' late an' he reckoned he'd turn in. He took us kids in the other room an' showed us where we'd sleep. When he struck a match I could see beddin' rolls layin' all about the room. Steve finally uncorded a roll for us. An' while Charlie struck matches so we could see he helped me spread it out. As soon as Steve got us kids fixed up he set down on a bed alongside of ours on the floor an' started pullin' off his boots.

It wasn't long before I heard Steve snore. But me an' Charlie was too spooky to go to sleep. For each time we started dozin' off, some puncher come in to bed. Each puncher struck a match to find his bed, an' most of them smoked a cigarette before they began to snore. The rain was still patterin' on the roof an' it was pretty stuffy in the room. But the longer I laid the wider awake I got. An' I finally asked Charlie, when they dipped us for ticks next day if he thought they'd dip us with all our clothes on.

"I don't know," he says, "for I ain't never seen nobody dipped for ticks before."

"Do you believe the yarn about the skunks?" I says.

"We're in a wild country now," he says, "an' we can expect most anythin'."

"I don't believe it anyway," I says. An' Charlie didn't say no more. But as soon as I figgered they was all asleep I got up an' shut the door an' put the window down.

"Purt Near!"

by

S. OMAR BARKER

They called him "Purt Near Perkins," for unless the booger lied,
He'd purt near done most everything that he had ever tried.
He'd purt near been a preacher and he'd purt near roped a bear;
He'd met up with Comanches once and purt near lost his hair.
He'd purt near wed an heiress who had money by the keg,
He'd purt near had the measles, and he'd purt near broke his leg.
He'd purt near been a trail boss, and accordin' to his claim,
He'd purt near shot Bill Hickok—which had purt near won him fame!
He'd purt near rode some broncs upon which no one else had stuck—
In fact he was the feller who had purt near drowned the duck!

Now mostly all the cowboys on the Lazy S B spread,
They took his talkin' with a grin and let him fight his head.
But one named Tom Maginnis sorter told it to him rough:
"You're riding' with an outfit now where 'purt near' ain't enough!
We tie our lass ropes to the horn, an' what we ketch we hold,
And 'purt near' is one alibi we never do unfold!
In fact, right now I'll tell you that no word I ever hear
Sounds quite so plain damn useless as that little pair: 'purt near'!"
That's how ol' Tom Maginnis laid it out upon the line,

And like a heap of preachin' talk, it sounded mighty fine.
But one day Tom Maginnis, while a-ridin' off alone,
He lamed his horse and had to ketch some neighbor nester's roan
To ride back to the ranch on. But somewhere along the way
A bunch of nesters held him up, and there was hell to pay!
Tom claimed he hadn't stole the horse—just borrowed it to ride.
Them nesters hated cowboys, and they told him that he lied.
They cussed him for a horsethief and they'd caught him with the goods.
They set right out to hang him in a nearby patch of woods.
They had pore Tom surrounded, with their guns all fixed to shoot.
It looked like this pore cowboy sure had heard his last owl hoot!
They tied a rope around his neck and throwed it o'er a limb,
And Tom Maginnis purt near knowed this was the last of him.
Then suddenly a shot rang out from somewhere up the hill!
Them nesters dropped the rope an' ran, like nesters sometimes will
When bullets start to whizzin'. Tom's heart lept up with hope
To see ol' Purt Near Perkins ridin' towards him at a lope.
"Looks like I purt near got here just in time," ol' Perkins said,
"To see them nesters hang you!" Tom's face got kinder red.

"You purt near did!" he purt near grinned. "They purt near had me strung!
You're lookin' at a cowboy that has purt near just been hung!
And also one that's changed his mind—for no word ever said,
Can sound as sweet as 'purt near', when a man's been purt near dead!"

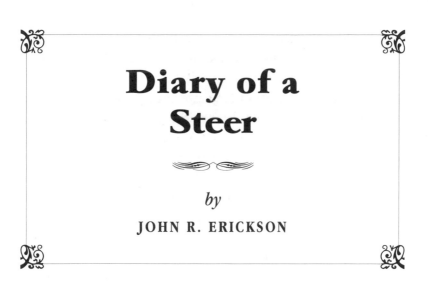

Diary of a Steer

by

JOHN R. ERICKSON

O CTOBER 1, 1978: Spent most of the day in a cattle truck. I can't say much for the accommodations. It was crowded and noisy.

The fellow standing next to me was originally from Alabama, a tall thin guy with big horns and a long cowy head. He said we're going to the Texas Panhandle where the grass is always too short and the winters too long. He wanted to go back to Alabam and he bawled for three straight hours.

I got sick and tired of hearing him. Finally I told him, "Listen, pal, I've never seen Alabam but I've seen you, and I don't want to go there." That shut him up for a while.

Around five o'clock we unloaded at a set of corrals. I can't see much of the country from here, but it appears there's a little creek to the south and some cliffs and canyons up north. It's hot and dusty in this country, but I'm not complaining. We got some good grub tonight, sweet feed and alfalfa. The hay was put up too dry, but it's got a good flavor.

Next day: This place is all right. I didn't do anything today but eat and drink. Went from the feed bunk to the hay feeder. When this got boring, I wandered over to the water tank. This is the life.

Even old Alabam filled up. He's not such a bad looking fellow after all. If you shortened his nose and tail by three feet, he'd pass for handsome.

We've got two cowboys taking care of us, John and Tom. Several times today they walked through the pen and looked us over. Just before sundown they brought in some more alfalfa hay. The food is excellent here, but these lots are awfully dusty. My allergies bothered me all day.

Next day: We had some trouble last night. One of the little guys came down with galloping pneumonia and died. John and Tom dragged him off with a pickup, and when they came back they went to work on us. They walked through the pen and when they found someone who looked thin or droopy, they cut him into the sick pen.

I was standing over by the water tank, minding my own business and chewing my cud. I got some dust up my nose and coughed, and the next thing I knew I was in the sick pen. They ran me into a chute, and while one of them stuck me in rump with needles, the other one poked three big white pills down my guzzle.

Next day: I spent the night in the sick pen with all the scrubs. This is outrageous. I've never received such shabby treatment in my life. They gave me more shots and pills today, even though I'm not sick.

All I did was cough at the wrong time. Who wouldn't cough in all this dust? Even John and Tom were coughing today. I wish I could get those two in the doctoring chute for about fifteen minutes.

Next day: Well, I got out of the sick pen today. I've learned one thing from this experience: don't cough when those two needle-happy cowboys are around.

Two days later: Yesterday the cowboys sorted us up into two bunches. My bunch was branded and turned out into the home pasture. We've got good grass and plenty of space. No more dust. I feel wonderful.

Next day: I don't feel so good today. Must be my allergies acting up.

Next day: I feel lousy. Maybe it's a sinus infection.

Next day: This ain't sinus. I'm sick. My nose is running and my ears are drooped so low I think they might fall off. I'm lying down in some sunflowers near the back side of the pasture. The cowboys rode by yesterday on horses. I had the feeling that they were looking for me, but they didn't see me.

Next day: They found me. They tried to drive me to the corrals but I wasn't in the mood for that. I wanted to sleep and be left alone. I went about a hundred yards and quit. When they tried to crowd me, I went after their horses. I guess I showed them a thing or two. They rode back to the house. I'm a pretty tough customer when I get mad. Gave those boys quite a scare. I doubt if they'll mess with me again.

Later that day: I underestimated the cowboys. They came back with a pickup and stock trailer. One of them stuck a rope on my neck and dragged me into the trailer with a big sorrel horse. If I'd been feeling better, I would have put up a better fight. Ordinarily, two cowboys are no match for me, and there isn't a horse alive that can push me around when I'm healthy. But I was feeling puny.

A week later: Spent a week in the sick pen. Every time I coughed or belched, one of those cowboys was coming at me with a needle or a pill. But I survived all their doctoring and I'm back in the home pasture.

I ran into Alabam today. The guy looks just as sorry as he did the day he got here. He's the worst looking steer in the bunch, but he hasn't spent a single day in the sick pen. That really hacks me off.

A week later: Lost my horns today. It happened so fast I didn't know it was coming. If I had, I might very well have destroyed the corrals in a display of brute strength. They ran me into a chute, put the squeeze to me, and then—crunch, no more horns. Sometimes I think Tom and John don't like steers.

Next day: Alabam lost his horns too and he bawled all night long.

It hurt his pride. Two days ago, he was nothing but horns and back-bone. Now he's nothing but backbone walking around on four legs.

Ten days later: The cowboys have left us alone since they knocked off our horns. Every day or two they'll ride past on horses and make us stand up and walk around. Those guys are so dumb they have to write their tally down in the palm of their hands. My cough is gone and I'm feeling much better.

Next day: Big doings today. The cowboys rounded up the home pasture. Me and Alabam gave them a run for their money. We got out in the lead and headed for the creek when they were trying to drive us into the corrals. Had a heck of a good time.

I learned something about Texas cowboys. They're pretty good hands ahorseback, but they're even better at cursing. They called us everything but nice before they got us gathered up.

When we finally gave up and went into the pens, the cowboys sorted off seventy-five of the best steers to go to wheat pasture. I, being the very handsomest of the bunch, was selected early. Some-how Alabam made the cut and he'll be going too.

Next day, November 10: We're on wheat pasture today. The country around here is as flat as a table, and looking in all directions I see nothing but luscious green wheat. I shall try to eat it all myself.

Next day: I tried to eat it all myself and came down with a belly-ache. I puffed up like a toad and could hardly walk. The cowboys came by this morning and ran a rubber hose down my guzzle. That was undignified, but I feel much better now.

Four days later: Alabam and I got bored yesterday. We looked across the fence and decided that the wheat was better over there. He showed me how to hop over an electric fence, and off we went. We ate and walked, walked and ate. Never had so much fun. Old Alabam knows how to have a good time. Last night he suggested that we hit the road and head for the Deep South. He has lots of friends down there. That sounded like a good idea.

But this morning our cowboys friends showed up with a stock

trailer and two horses. They wanted us to go back to the wheat field but we declined their invitation. We headed south in a dead run.

Must have made the cowboys mad because they cursed us and pulled down their ropes. They caught both of us and tied us to utility poles, then they went back to the trailer.

Tom was riding that same sorrel horse that stuck me in the trailer last summer. I decided he wasn't going to do it again. I braced all four feet and fought like a panther. Sometimes I'm amazed by my own strength. I wasn't going to let them put me in that trailer.

But you know what? They did. That sorrel son of a gun jerked me out of my tracks and threw me into the trailer so hard that I scabbed my nose on the front end. Then they did the same thing to Alabam. They gave him such a jerk that I think they lengthened his backbone by a full six inches.

I guess we'll stay home from now on.

A week later, November 24: Boy, it was hot today. Alabam said it was supposed to be cold in the Panhandle. He was wrong. It's been hot as blazes. Alabam is a nice fellow but he's a little short on brains.

Next day: It's snowing. The wind is blowing forty miles an hour. I have a big icicle handing on the end of my nose. Alabam cried all night long. He wants to go home. I want to go with him.

Last night, when the wind was blowing snow into our faces, he said something that I thought was kind of interesting. He was moaning about the cold and said something like, "It was a lot better in my former life."

I said, what do you mean, in your former life? And he said he'd been on this earth before, only then he wasn't a skinny steer. I said, well, what the heck were you? And he said, "A cowboy in the Texas Panhandle. I got sent to hell, but Satan said that was too good for me, so they sent me back to the Panhandle as a steer."

I don't know whether to believe him or not. But if he's right about this, then Tom and John are in for a rude surprise.

The Disgraceful Affair of Turpentine Jackson

by

BENJAMIN CAPPS

T O THE PRESIDENT OF THE COMPANY and other officers, Dear Mr. Blackmoor:

First, they say it is a disgraceful affair, which I don't say is true, and hope it don't reflect on the good name of the Blackmoor Land and Cattle Company. As to giving the account, this is what I have to respectfully say for the record and to put it in black and white. I think Mr. Jackson's name is Henry, as I found it put down H. Jackson, but as you know he answers to the name of Turpentine. I want to apply and say that because I paid him twice I don't think it should be deducted from my salary. This is in the amount of sixty dollars cash money. I was told and instructed many times when out of contact with superior officers of the Company, to use my own judgment, which I did to the best of my ability.

I had them put me down as Acting Foreman McWhirter, since I did not know if I have been promoted or not. Anyway, this here's a copy of the agreement or contract, so as you can understand what went on.

AGREEMENT

Whereas, it being the determination of the following various partics to scttle certain serious grievances and alleged crimes and debts and damages once and for all, we the contracting parties hereto do agree and affirm:

That the party of the first part shall include the Honorable Mayor of the City of Dodge City, the Chief of Police of the City of Dodge City, the High Sheriff of Ford County, the aforesaid Sheriff also as a representative of the State of Kansas, the Commanding Officer of Fort Dodge, the President of the Chamber of Commerce of the City of Dodge City, and the Secretary of the Civic Improvement League of the City of Dodge City.

Further, that the party of the second part shall include, but not be limited to, Elmore McWhirter, Acting Foreman of the Blackmoor Land and Cattle Company, having authority over Turpentine Jackson, all owners and operators of said Cattle Company having authority over the employee Turpentine Jackson, and any keepers or guardians having influence or control over the aforesaid Turpentine Jackson.

Now whereas it is agreed that herein claims do not represent final judgments in either civil or criminal actions, the party of the first part does nevertheless present an itemized statement of account, to wit:

One bowl of chili at Welcome Tex Café. Not paid for .... .10
Defamatory and libelous statement of finding dog hair in
chili at Welcome Tex Café $5.00
Fee for cleaning wall, Welcome Tex Café .... .50
Four drinks first-class whiskey at Cowboy Oasis. Not paid for . .80
Libelous and defamatory statement calling first-class whiskey at
Cowboy Oasis epithet approx. "liquid mule waste." Damages ... $2.00
Grabbing money back improperly from Slick Hendricks,
sporting man and part owner of Cowboy Oasis $7.00

Calling Slick Hendricks "crooked as rail fence" and also
"crooked as dog's hind leg" at Cowboy Oasis. Damages
to reputation of Slick Hendricks $5.00
Referring to occupation of Hog Nose Kate in public
and making disparaging remarks about professional
competence. Mental anguish and damage to reputation
of Hog Nose Kate $1.00
One large mirror, Cowboy Oasis. Replacement cost $14.00
Failure to halt at first order by officer of law, to wit:
City Marshal Owen Sims. Fine....................................... $3.00
Resisting arrest. Fine $3.00
Court costs, if tried, above two counts, $1.00 per count $2.00
Damages to Marshal Sims's firearm $4.00
Sending Peewee Hawkins down in city well to retrieve
firearm. Cost.. $1.00
Striking City Marshal in eye while in performance of his
duty. Fine... $3.00
One pound beefsteak.. .10
Four yards cotton bandage .... .20
Five drinks first-class whiskey, Eddie's Emporium. Not
paid for.. $1.00
Insulting and defamatory remarks about Eddie. Damages $4.00
Public statement that Mayor J. B. Krenshaw cheats at
poker and is bigger crook than Slick Hendricks. Severe
mental anguish and damage to reputation, also
contempt of elected official... $7.00
Calling New Orleans Rose epithet while she was verbally
defending elected official. Also making lewd and suggestive
references. Damage to reputation of New Orleans Rose $1.00
Breaking plate glass over large art picture of "Venus
Bathing with Maidens," Eddie's Emporium. Cost................ $9.00
Drunk and disorderly, including statement that Turpentine
Jackson can whip Mayor and two soldiers. Fine................ $3.00

Making reference to mother of Mayor. Damage to
reputation and good name of mother of Mayor Krenshaw $7.00
Fighting on public streets, namely Front Street by
Cattlemen's Hotel. Fine $3.00
One window, Cattlemen's Hotel. Cost $1.00
Assault and battery against two soldiers, to wit: one
corporal and one private. Fine $3.00
Resisting arrest by Deputy Sheriff Perkins. Fine $3.00
Calling one corporal and one private "Yankee" plus epithet
denying marriage of parents. Damage to reputations $2.00
Two gold teeth of Deputy Sheriff Perkins. $4.00 per tooth $8.00
Three stitches in nose of aforesaid Perkins, seven
stitches in mouth. Doctor's fee $2.00
Miscellaneous damage to signs of retail establishments
along Front Street, including one barber pole ruined $1.50
Refusing to halt at request of three duly constituted
officers of the law, to wit: Chief of Police Webbington,
Sheriff Trueblood, and Constable Orr. Fine $3.00
Continuing to resist arrest, after warning. Fine $3.00
False, misleading, and defamatory remarks about
aforesaid officers $4.50
Sheriff Trueblood's pocket watch. Damages..................... $9.00
Constable Orr's spectacles. Damages........................... $6.00
Chief Webbington's coat, sleeve torn and pocket ripped
out. Damages..................... $1.50
Damage to bench in front of City Jail $1.25
Miscellaneous derogatory and malicious statements
about officials, employees, and citizens of the City of
Dodge City, and also the State of Kansas, including U.S.
Army personnel stationed therein $8.00
Damages inside City Jail, including, but not limited to,
one sprung door, one mattress, and toilet facilities............ $24.00
Three counts of Contempt of Court before Justice of the

Peace Adcock, $3.00 per count $9.00
False and defamatory statement that said Turpentine
Jackson can whip Justice of the Peace Adcock $2.50
One pound beefsteak.. .10
Six yards cotton bandage .... .30

GRAND TOTAL of damages, fines, costs, unpaid bills $179.35

Minus $4.00 credited to said Jackson for one gold tooth
discovered following morning in chamber pot, Miller's
Boarding House, and returned to owner....................... $4.00

BALANCE $175.35

Withdrawal of damage claim to reputation of Hog Nose
Kate plus statement that Turpentine Jackson is a good
man at heart. (Opinion only.) Also statement of Civic
Improvement League that said Hog Nose Kate is not
a nice person. (Opinion only.)

WITHDRAWAL OF CLAIM $1.00

FINAL BALANCE $174.35

Now, whereas, the representatives of Turpentine Jackson decline
to submit an itemized account of any monies owing to him, the following statement by said Jackson is incorporated as part of the agreement herein: "I know [expletive] I had sixty dollars, two whole
months' pay, when I came into this [four expletives] town. I sure did-
n't spend it, and I got only twenty-five [expletive] cents now."

Further, in answer to the above, Justice of the Peace Adcock
swears and affirms that said Jackson had only twenty-five cents on
him when he was admitted to the City Jail; and said Adcock says two

residents of the City Jail, namely Joe Lefors and Charles Blankenship, saw that the aforesaid Turpentine Jackson had only twenty-five cents, and he can prove it by the said witnesses.

Further, whereas Acting Foreman Elmore McWhirter of the Blackmoor Land and Cattle Company says he only wants to do a good turn and make peace between the parties involved, he, the aforesaid McWhirter, affirms that the Blackmoor Land and Cattle Company takes responsibility for acts of employees only when they are doing assigned duties for the said Company. And further he swears and affirms that he did pay Turpentine Jackson sixty dollars in cash money, and does not know whether Jackson got his money's worth in recreational benefits.

Therefore, whereas no full statement and itemized account is forthcoming from the party of the second part, it is agreed as follows, to wit: The aforesaid Jackson did enter the City Limits of the City of Dodge City with the said sixty dollars; and that subsequent to his entry the money was taken from him, legally or illegally, by person or persons unknown.

Furthermore, whereas various claims are made herein, but not admitted, if one principal condition shall be met, then all debts, damages, fines, and similar charges shall be canceled and forgiven. The principal condition being thus, namely, to wit: that the party of the second part, in particular Acting Foreman McWhirter, but including the owners and operators of the Blackmoor Land and Cattle Company and all persons who may have any control, authority, or influence over the aforesaid Jackson, either now or in the future, shall immediately and forthwith remove the said Jackson from the vicinity of the City of Dodge City. Further, they, the aforesaid party of the second part, shall prevent said Jackson from entering back into said City Limits at any time in the future, either south of the tracks or north of the tracks, nor shall he be allowed to approach the military reservation of Fort Dodge or any personnel stationed thereon. Further they, the aforesaid party of the second party, shall prevent the said Jackson from entering Ford County; and further they shall prevent said Jackson from entering the State of Kansas.

And be it further agreed that Acting Foreman McWhirter and others, should Turpentine Jackson quit the employment of the Blackmoor Land and Cattle Company and thereby come out from under their control, authority, and influence, then Acting Foreman McWhirter and others, if they believe the said Jackson is heading for Kansas, shall notify the proper officials by telegram.

In witness whereof, we, the various parties of the various parts, do affix our signatures in good faith and in the presence of a Notary Public.

END OF AGREEMENT

Well, Mr. Blackmoor, that's the facts as requested, and I admit I signed the agreement for the Company, as I was told and instructed many times when out of contact with my superiors in the Company to use my own judgment, which I did to the best of my ability. I was also asked to make suggestions for the profit and good name of my employers whenever I deemed I ought to, so here goes: We could ship at Denison, Texas, or go plum past Dodge and up to Ogallala, Nebraska, next spring. Sir, there is a rough and rowdy element at Dodge City, which comes from the uneducated buffalo skinners and soldiers and teamsters and such types as gamblers, as well as some that is highly placed officials, and this is a bad influence on cowhands.

I hope this gives to you the explanation in black and white as requested, and respectfully say I don't think you should dock me the sixty dollars.

Yrs. Truly,
ELMORE McWHIRTER
Acting Foreman

The Legend of Boastful Bill

by

CHARLES BADGER CLARK, JR.

At a round-up on the Gila
One sweet morning long ago,
Ten of us was throwed quite freely
By a hoss from Idaho.
An' we 'lowed he'd go a-beggin'
For a man to break his pride
Till, a-hitchin' up one leggin',
Boastful Bill cut loose an' cried:
"I'm a ornery proposition for to hurt,
I fulfil my earthly mission with a quirt,
I can ride the highest liver
'Twixt the Gulf an' Powder River,
An' I'll break this thing as easy as I'd flirt."

So Bill climbed the Northern fury
An' they mangled up the air
Till a native of Missouri
Would have owned the brag was fair.
Though the plunges kept him reelin'
An' the wind it flapped his shirt,

Loud above the hoss's squealin'
We could hear our friend assert:
"I'm the one to take such rockin's as a joke;
Someone hand me up the makin's of a smoke.
If you think my fame needs brightnin',
Why, I'll rope a streak o' lightnin'
An' spur it up an' quirt it till it's broke."

Then one caper of repulsion
Broke that hoss's back in two,
Cinches snapped in the convulsion,
Skyward man and saddle flew,
Up they mounted, never flaggin',
And we watched them through our tears,
While this last, thin bit o' braggin'
Came a-floatin' to our ears:
"If you ever watched my habits very close,
You would know I broke such rabbits by the gross.
I have kept my talent hidin',
I'm too good for earthly ridin',
So I'm off to bust the lightnin'—Adios!"

Years have passed since that ascension;
Boastful Bill ain't never lit;
So we reckon he's a-wrenchin'
Some celestial outlaw's bit.
When the night wind flaps our slickers,
And the rain is cold and stout,
And the lightnin' flares and flickers,
We can sometimes hear him shout:
"I'm a ridin' son o' thunder o' the sky,
I'm a broncho twistin' wonder on the fly.
Hey, you earthlin's, shut your winders,

We're a-rippin' clouds to flinders.
If this blue-eyed darlin' kicks at you, you die."

Star-dust on his chaps and saddle,
Scornful still of jar and jolt,
He'll come back sometime a-straddle
Of a bald-faced thunderbolt;
And the thin-skinned generation
Of that dim and distant day
Sure will stare with admiration
When they hear old Boastful say:
"I was first, as old raw-hiders all confest,
I'm the last of all rough riders, and the best.
Huh! you soft and dainty floaters
With your aeroplanes and motors,
Huh! are you the greatgrandchildren of the West?"

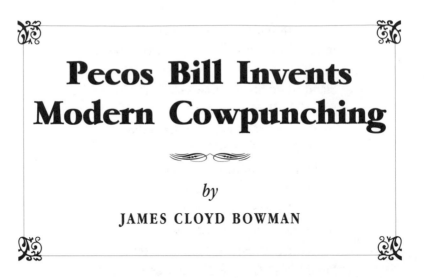

Pecos Bill Invents Modern Cowpunching

by

JAMES CLOYD BOWMAN

ALL THE MEN OF THE I. X. L. were eating out of Pecos Bill's hand within less than a week after he arrived. He took to the life of a cowboy like a duck to water. He learned their best tricks, then went on to do better. Gun Smith and Chuck and the rest were very soon like children before him. Among themselves, they bragged about their noble deeds; but when Pecos was around, they couldn't help thinking that they were mere bridled cayuses.

He could stand on the ground beside a broncho, turn an air flop, and land astride the pony before it had time to tighten a muscle. He could ride bareback without a bridle. He could urge his pony at top speed over ground so rough and uneven that Gun Smith and the others were afraid even to attempt it with bit and saddle. And he was so casual and modest about everything he did that they thought Pecos the eighth wonder of the world. Almost at once he was full of ideas. And what ideas!

Up to Pecos Bill's day, when a man wanted to capture a horse or a steer, he would lay a piece of rope down on the ground, make a loop in one end of it, sit down behind a tree or a blind, and by laying a bait, try to coax the wild critter to step within the loop. He would then jerk sharply on the rope, and perhaps one time in a dozen, if he was lucky, he would succeed in making a catch. It was no uncommon thing for a man to wait around and lose an entire month's time without laying hold of a single animal.

"Well, this sort of thing has got to be changed," said Pecos Bill to himself when no one was near to hear him. "A man can't be expected to waste his entire lifetime catching a single horse or cow."

Without further delay, Pecos got hold of the longest piece of rope he could find around the ranch, and began to throw it through the air. Next he rode off alone where the others could not see what he was doing. After three days of constant practice, he found that he could lasso almost anything. He was limited only by the reach of his line.

Pecos Bill would just make a large loop in one end of his rope, swing it wildly about his head three or four times, and then, with a quick flip of his forearm and wrist, send it flying like a bullet. And as he grew more and more skilled, he added rapidly to the length of his rope.

As soon as he was entirely sure of himself, Pecos asked the boys to come out and let him show them his new invention.

"See that roan steer across there? That's Old Crook-horn, our wildest critter, ain't it?" Pecos asked quietly.

Before anyone was aware of what he was doing, Pecos had whirled his loop about his head and had sent it so fast in the direction of the four-year-old, that the eye could scarcely follow it.

In an instant the old steer began to jump and bellow, and Pecos Bill to tow in the rope. Soon the astonished steer stood with lowered head before the even more surprised cowboys.

Not content with this great skill, Pecos began practicing from horseback.

In another week, he again called his cowboys out to see what he could do. They watched, with popping eyes, as he gave his rope a double turn around his saddle-bow. He then started his broncho at a hard gallop. They saw him quickly approach a rather tall, scraggly mesquite tree, whirl his loop wildly about his head and then fling it into the air. When he dragged a great hawk down from the topmost branch with the noose about its neck, the men were unable to believe their eyes.

"What sort o' wonder worker is this anyway?" they asked each other. "No human could ever throw the rope like that!"

Then Pecos Bill showed the men how it was done, and after two or three months of hard practice, each of them was able to make frequent catches at a distance of from ten to not more than twenty feet.

In the meantime, Pecos Bill had become dissatisfied with the fact that he couldn't find a longer rope. So he began to braid himself a cowhide lariat. This is how he went to work. First he looked up some old horned steers that had lived so many years within the depths of the trees that there were green algae on their backs—moss-backs, sure enough. What's more, these steers were so old their faces were gray and wrinkled.

Whenever Pecos Bill got hold of one of these old fellows, he first loosened the hide behind the ears. He then grasped the steer by the tail and with a flip of his wrist and forearm and a wild yowl, he frightened the animal so that it jumped out of its skin. The tough hides of these old moss-backs were just what Pecos needed.

Three or four years later when he had it finished, his loyal ranchers declared on all sides that the lariat was as long as the equator, and that Pecos could lasso anything this side of China.

It was thus that Pecos Bill solved one of the problems that had worried cowhands and their bosses for years.

Another thing that Pecos very soon learned was that every ranch outfit was a bitter enemy of every other outfit. When two neighboring ranchers happened to meet anywhere near the supposed boundary of their pastures lands, they would begin to complain about missing cattle. Soon one would accuse the other of rustling—a polite word for stealing—his stock. Then there would be a sudden flashing of pistols, and one or the other, and often both men would bite the dust.

"Why do they all make such fools of themselves?" Pecos Bill asked. "Why don't they invent some way of marking their horses and cattle so that they will know them wherever they happen to meet them? All this fighting and killing is sheer nonsense. The spirit of the Coyote pack is entirely lacking."

While Pecos Bill was trying to invent a plan for marking the animals, a deer fly gave him just the right suggestion when it nipped him sharply on the arm. In chasing the fly away, he just naturally happened to notice the tattooed star that was his own mark of identification. "Mother was wiser than all these cowmen put together," Pecos declared, laughing at himself for having been so slow in finding the right idea! "Why of course cattle and horses can be tattooed the same way. Then they'll be marked for life."

That very evening Pecos Bill explained his plans to Bean Hole. The cook listened, then shook his head. "But tattooin' is too infernal slow," declared Bean Hole, looking at the purple markings up and down the backs of his own arms. "It wasted more'n a whole week of my time to do these pictures. It'd be quicker to burn the mark on. I ain't been cookin' all these years for nothin'. I know that if you burn the skin deep enough, it'll leave an everlastin' scar. Look at this mark now—I've been carryin' it on my wrist for more'n twenty-seven years, and it's just as plain now as ever it was."

"You're right," shouted Pecos. "Together we've invented a new system of bookkeeping for every cowhand in the world."

That evening Pecos explained the new invention to the cowboys, who were open-mouthed at the cleverness of the plan. Rusty Peters, who was a blacksmith by trade, was set immediately to make the brands. He bent the iron so that it would read I X L when burnt upon the side of a horse or a cow.

The next morning all the men were as excited as boys. They

herded and roped the cattle, dragging them near the heated irons and throwing them on their side to apply the stinging brand. All day long the smoke curled. All day long the cattle bellowed.

"Keep that iron a cherry red, I'm a-tellin' you," shouted Bean Hole, as he gave directions. "Hold it on long enough to do more'n singe the hair. Wait till it smells like the Devil's own stithy, and looks like the whole critter was burned to a cracklin'. That's not near long enough. She'll shed that mark before the snow flies. There, that's about right. Let her bawl her fill. The loss of a few mouthfuls of hot air ain't going to hurt her any."

"Keep quiet, you old bag o' wind," shouted Rusty Peters, hard at work. "I ain't a blacksmith for nothin'! I'll burn a brand across your mouth in a minute if you don't keep quiet."

By evening the entire job was completed. It was found that the I. X. L. outfit possessed fifty-seven steers of various ages, forty-one cows, some fat and sleek, some spindly and thin, and twenty-four calves.

"This small herd ain't really enough to bother with," Pecos Bill observed in disappointment. "I thought you cowmen said you had a real ranch. Why, the woods are full of wild cattle that belong to nobody in particular. I'll just go out and drive in a few thousand of them. We'll put our trademark on them, and then they'll be ours."

"But how in tarnation will we ever keep these longhorns from runnin' straight away again?" asked Gun Smith with doubting stare. "What's the use of goin' through all this trouble disfigurin' the sides of all these cattle with our silly I. X. L. advertisement, if we're goin' to turn 'em back to the wild prairies again?"

Pecos Bill had not thought of this. The general custom among the cowmen had been to allow all the cattle to go and come whenever they liked. The ranch shack was nearly always built beside running water, and naturally, a few of the timid and lazy cows and steers would make this their home. The more ambitious stock would just as naturally wander off across the prairies and mesa and take refuge within the mesquite woods. Soon they would be as wild as deer and as difficult to catch.

This careless way of doing things meant that each ranch had a mere handful of shifting population, as far as the cattle were concerned. When the pasture and the water elsewhere were scarce, the cattle would flock to the ranch; but most of the time they would not even trouble themselves to take a French leave.

"It's dead wrong," said Pecos Bill to himself as he squatted on his haunches. "The problem to be solved is this: How are the cattle to be kept together in a herd after they are branded?"

While he was trying to work out the answer, he loped off alone to the top of a small mountain one morning before the others were awake. Far over the rolling prairies he could see many small wandering herds of cows and steers.

"Of course, if bad should come to worse, I could just round the herd up every night and throw my noose about them, and tie the cattle up till morning," he smiled. "But that ain't a good solution, for I can't bind myself that close to the ranch. I've got to reserve my energy for bigger work. All kinds of things are waiting to be invented."

At first as he sat and thought, his mind was just one grazing herd after another. He saw cattle scattered all over the prairies; he saw cattle stampeded, and he saw cattle leaving the herd to get lost in the wild mesa. But after a little things cleared up and he knew what he was going to do.

He got up, stretched the kinks out of his muscles and started at a brisk gallop for the ranch house. As soon as he arrived he called out for everybody to come.

"Here's the plan," he said excitedly. "The way to keep the herd together is for you men to ride out with the cattle every day. By waking up the drags and by holding back the leaders, the herd can be kept together and can be made to go to the best feeding grounds every day."

"You mean," said Gun Smith, with an ironical smile, "that us cowpunchers has got to be ordinary bovine critters the rest of our lives?"

"And stay with the herd all night and sleep with the hoot-owl?" asked Moon Hennessey sourly.

"Oh, yes," and the musical Mushmouth sang with a pretense of tears in his voice:

"The centipede runs 'cross my head,
The vinegaroon crawls in my bed,
Tarantulas jump and scorpions play,
The bronchs are grazin' far away,
The rattlesnake sounds his noisy cry,
And the Coyotes sing their lullaby,
While I *sleep* soundly beneath the sky."

"It don't appeal to me," complained Moon Hennessey.

"Oh, well, you'll be just crazy about it when you've tried it—especially if the herd stampedes in your direction," suggested Gun Smith with irony. "It's goin' to be a regular picnic, Sundays and week days together, an' there's no doubt about it."

"And if the herd gets stampeded you'll be on hand to turn the leaders and start them milling until they are bitterly disappointed in trying to run away," added Pecos Bill quietly. "Besides, sleeping out under the stars is wonderful, once you've acquired the knack. I know from long experience."

"It'll all be easier than handlin' a month-old heifer calf," laughed Gun Smith bitterly.

"Well, now that we have decided what to do, I'll go out and drive in the cattle to be branded. And while I'm away Gun Smith will be your foreman. He'll keep you out of mischief. We can't get started too soon. So, with your permission, I'll be going right away. I'll have a herd ready to be branded first thing in the morning."

As soon as Pecos Bill had darted out into the night, the men began to wonder whether his coming to them had been a blessing or a curse.

"Chuck, before this monstrosity of yours arrived," began Moon Hennessey, "we was leadin' a peaceful and easy life. All we was expected to do was swap lies, and eat juicy tobacco. Now, it seems, we're goin' to be set at hard labor!"

"To my way of thinkin', the change will be all to the good," answered Chuck. "And who knows—it may bring us glory and honor—and gold!"

"Well, then, since I'm the appointed foreman of this outfit until Pecos returns," Gun Smith drawled as he put his hands on his guns, "I'm goin' to give you, Chuck, the place of highest honor. While the rest of us turn in for the night, you, Chuck, will take your Old Pepper and make contact with our branded herd. If they object to your presence and attempt to trample you and your noble steed to smithereens by startin' a wild stampede, you'll simply turn the leaders and set the herd millin'. If they show signs of thirst, you will lead them beside the still water!"

"Thank you very much for the honor," answered Chuck, as he rose promptly to carry out the assigned task.

"The rest of us motherless mavericks," Gun Smith continued, "will remain here, so's to be on hand with the ropes and the brandin' irons when Old Pecos returns any minute with his promised herd of wild cattle."

"Well," added Moon Hennessey with a bored yawn, "Old Pecos will be doin' splendid if he shows up by the end of next week. There'll be no herd here tomorrow mornin', I can promise you that."

"Don't fool yourself," replied Chuck spiritedly as he turned on his heel. "You evidently ain't yet acquainted with my brother."

"Brother!" fairly hissed Moon Hennessey in a rage. "Cut out your star identification talk and go on about your business!"

Next morning the men were awakened at early dawn by the dull thud, thud, thud of innumerable hoofs, and by the monotonous bawling of the weary cattle. As the men rubbed the sleep out of their eyes and looked about, they discovered, to their astonishment, that Pecos Bill had actually returned with a herd so large that they couldn't begin to see either its beginning or end.

"What, aren't you boys up yet?" Pecos called with a smile. "I've been having a wonderful night. And I've got enough cattle here to keep all of us busy for a while, anyway."

"Enough wild critters to keep the brandin' irons sizzlin' and the smoke risin' for a month of Sundays, I'd say," conceded Gun Smith, none too happily.

But Pecos Bill had no use for conversation just then. Breakfast was gulped down, cattle struggling and bellowing; the alkali dust flying mountain high; Bean Hole rushing about like a chicken with its head off, shouting his directions amid the din and waving his kettles and pans, and Rusty Peters keeping the smoking brands busy. This was the way it went all day long. By the time the sun had set, the tired men had added three hundred and thirty-eight cattle to their herd. Three hundred and thirty-eight—hurrah for Pecos Bill!

Pecos Bill himself was so happy over the results that frequently during the following months he would go out for an evening adventure, returning promptly the following morning with hundreds more bawling wild cattle. By the end of the season the I. X. L. ranch was one living sea of four-footed beasts.

As soon as his men had finished branding the incoming herd with the I. X. L. trademark, Pecos Bill at once began looking around to find other worlds to conquer. He instructed the men how to live in the saddle, and how to take cat naps astride their grazing ponies. He showed them how to soothe the cattle by crooning songs to them, and how to keep the herd together without annoying even the leaders.

When the herd stampeded, as it was sure to do at times, Pecos taught the men how to turn the leaders, and thus start the entire herd milling in a circle until the cattle finally winded themselves, and stopped through sheer weariness in the very spot from which they had started in the first place.

During these days, Bean Hole was the busiest man this side of Mars. After trying for a week to feed the men by carrying food out to them from the ranch shack, he finally gave up. On four or five different occasions, as he was starting out with his kettles and pans, he actually met himself on the trail coming back with the empty dishes of the previous afternoon. If he hadn't stopped his foolishness of trying to work twenty-seven hours a day just when he did, most likely his ghost would still be wandering on the wind over the same trails.

In the despair of complete exhaustion, Bean Hole finally hitched two spans of mules to the chuck wagon, loaded it down with enough food to last a fortnight, and left the ranch shack to take care of itself. He hadn't been gone half an hour before the place looked as deserted as the ruins of Pompeii.

Very soon the entire life of the ranch was going along according to the new plan. Everything was clicking like clock work and Pecos Bill was so pleased, for the present at least, that he couldn't think of anything left to invent. So he decided to go out and tell the world about what he had been doing, not for the sake of his own fame, but for the benefit of the cowmen of the entire range country.

One evening, after the cattle had settled down for the first sleep of the night, Pecos Bill announced to Gun Smith, his foreman, that it would be necessary for him to go away from the ranch for a few days. "If anybody asks where I am," he whispered, "just tell them that I'll be back for breakfast, like as not."

Pecos then took his boots under his arm, threw his coiled rope over his shoulder, and went bounding off across the rolling prairie.

When he came to a strange ranch, he would quickly put on his boots and walk in great dignity, with jangling spurs, up to the boss of the outfit. Very soon he would be telling the wide-eyed cowman his story. In this way he easily covered forty or fifty miles in an hour and a half or two hours.

Pecos Bill thus visited all the ranches of the entire Southwest within two or three months. Not forgetting a single detail, he told the men everywhere what he had done. At first they thought him the biggest liar that had ever been invented in the whole world of cowmen. But when he had limbered up his lariat, and when they had witnessed his performance, they were quite willing to believe everything he told them.

What they saw was even more wonderful than what he had said. For with perfect ease, he would lasso any animal within reach of their vision. He could lasso a grazing or galloping steer, or lay his flying noose around the neck of a bald eagle in full flight.

The flying visits led later to many heated disputes among the puzzled ranchers: "You say this Pecos Bill left Hub's Ferry at nine o'clock? But he was at Slippery Mike's by eleven, and that's a good forty miles as the crow flies, ain't it? And he was alone and on foot, wasn't he? Who is this Pecos Bill, anyway?" Every rancher seemed to have a bigger yarn to tell than his neighbor.

But they were all true—certainly! And through the efforts of Pecos Bill, ranchmen began to have a spring roundup and fall roundup. Pecos persuaded the ranchers of a given range section or river valley to drive together all the cattle of their entire district. They then sorted them into individual herds according to the particular brand of each owner. After this work was completed, each owner branded all of his calves. The strays, with no brand, and the orphan mavericks were then distributed equally and branded so that they could never again go astray. And every bit of the plan was Pecos Bill's.

In the fall the roundup was repeated so that the stray cattle could be located and given back to their rightful owners. After all the exchanges were made, the cowmen, as they took their herds back to their individual feeding grounds, found it easy to count the number of steers that were in condition for the market and the number that they would have to pasture during the coming winter.

Thus it was that each owner was given what belonged to him, according to the laws of reason, and not in accordance with the earlier outlawry of the pistol.

And so it came about very naturally, through the organization of all the scattered cowmen, that the fame of Pecos Bill rapidly spread to the four corners of the range country. From the valley of the Rio Grande, through Texas and New Mexico, Arizona and Colorado, Kansas and Nebraska, and far into the wilderness of Montana and Wyoming, cowboys, when they met, would carelessly throw one foot free from its stirrup and in a resting position shout to their nearest companion: "Say, have you heard about the rope Uncle Bill is still braidin' down on the Pecos? Why, it's already twice as long as the equator! You know, if Old Pecos Bill could only get a toe hold on the moon, he'd turn in and lasso this wanderin' planet of ours and bring it back into the Milky Way, where it belongs! Yes, and Pecos could do it easier than you or I could lasso a year-old heifer calf!"

The Cloud
Puncher

by

WILLIAM CUNNINGHAM

A WHILE BEFORE THE CYCLONE SEASON, a man with uncommon bow legs arrived and said people usually called him Parenthesis, he didn't know why. He said he would work for the outfit if we furnished a horse.

The foreman said that was real kind of him, and what kind of a horse would he like.

Parenthesis said it made no difference, only he preferred a spirited mount.

The foreman said we've got a spirited mount. The only trouble was he bucks a little when you first get on.

Parenthesis said it made no difference, only he liked one with spirits.

The foreman winked at us and said ketch up the piebald and put the gentleman's saddle on it.

We looked at each other with great surprise, because the last man that tried to ride the piebald was throwed so high that he turned three summersets before he hit the ground. We saddled the piebald. There wasn't nothing wrong with him except he had some cockleburs in his mane and tail.

Parenthesis mounted and took off his hat and waved it and we run to get out of the way. The piebald fooled around for a while, jumping about ten feet in the air and coming down stiff-legged, figuring to jar the rider's teeth out of his upper jaw if he didn't have his mouth shut when they landed. But Parenthesis kept his mouth shut, and so the piebald went to work. He arose straight up and switched ends in midair, figuring to twist the rider's head off if he didn't have a strong neck. But Parenthesis kept his head, and after a half-hour of this, the piebald got tired.

Parenthesis dismounted. When we unsaddled the piebald we noticed he had bucked all the cockleburs out of his mane and tail.

Parenthesis said the piebald would do, unless the outfit had a horse with more spirits. The foreman said well we've got a spirited mount. The only trouble was he bucks a little when you first get on, if you don't mind that.

Parenthesis said he didn't mind.

The foreman winked at us and said saddle the pinto.

We looked at each other with dismay because the last man that tried to ride the pinto got a bad sunburn through the seat of his pants before he hit the ground, his pants being a little threadbare and the sun shining through the cloth. We saddled the pinto. There wasn't nothing wrong with him except he had some of these stick-tight fleas in his ears.

Parenthesis mounted and took off his hat and waved it and we run to get out of the way. The pinto fooled around for a while, jumping about fifteen feet in the air and coming down stiff-legged so hard that he buried his feet in the ground up to the ankles. Then he went straight up and twisted himself in midair, so that his front feet was pointing straight down and his hind feet pointing straight up. This was to throw the rider off balance. But Parenthesis kept his balance and after a half-hour of this the pinto got tired.

Parenthesis dismounted. When we unsaddled the pinto we noticed he had bucked all the fleas out of his ears.

Parenthesis said the pinto would do, unless the outfit had a horse with more spirits. The foreman said well we've got a spirited mount. The only trouble was he bucks a little when you first get on, if you don't mind that.

Parenthesis said he didn't mind that.

The foreman winked at us and said saddle the strawberry roan.

We looked at each other with consternation because the last man that tried to ride the strawberry roan, a couple of sparrows built a nest in his navel. We saddled the strawberry roan. There wasn't nothing wrong with him.

Parenthesis mounted and took off his hat and waved it and we run. The piebald fooled around for a while, jumping about twenty feet in the air and coming down stiff-legged so hard that he buried his feet in the ground up to the knees. Then he went straight up and we never did know just what he done. He seemed to kind of explode into a strawberry roan cloud and then he fell out of the cloud stark naked. He made some kind of a twist up there so sudden that he bucked off all his own hair, including the long hairs in his tail and mane. But he couldn't shake off Parenthesis, so after a half-hour he quit.

Parenthesis said the strawberry roan would do, and he went to work for our outfit. Every time he got on that strawberry roan, they went cavorting off across the alkali, and whatever hair the strawberry roan grew overnight he bucked off the next morning.

You would think Parenthesis would get his spine jarred often enough on a horse like that, but he didn't. He always wanted to ride something that bucked. He would pick out the orneriest, longest-legged steer in a herd and ride up beside him and jump off his horse onto the steer's back, and away they'd go, Parenthesis waving his hat. He didn't seem to need no surcingle, like most fellers do on a steer, or turn around and ride backwards, holding to the tail. You know how a steer is. Seems his hind legs is so much longer than his front legs that you just naturally slide down on his horns. But Parenthesis didn't seem to slide.

The cyclones was bad that year. Every once in a while we'd see one off a little distance, like a big funnel in the sky. It would settle to the ground and suck up everything on the ground for a ways and then lift and travel high for a few miles.

Well one day just when Parenthesis got on his naked horse, a cyclone dipped down. We all fell flat on our faces and dug our fingers into the grass roots to keep from being pulled up. Then we looked up, and there went Parenthesis about a thousand feet in the air, waving his hat. And the naked horse was standing there looking up with the most astonished look you ever seen on the face of a horse, and a grief-stricken look too. I think he was sorry to see Parenthesis taken off that way.

We was all sorry, but we agreed if Parenthesis had to go, that was the best way, up in the sky, waving his hat.

Some said the naked strawberry roan had managed to toss Parenthesis into the air at last and the cyclone took him from there. Others said the cyclone pulled him out of the saddle. We didn't know.

Some thought the cyclone would drop him astraddle of a barbed wire fence and split him lengthways. Some said it would slide him through one along the ground, slicing him like a boloney. We looked for him far and wide but didn't find hide nor hair of him, either split or sliced.

Then one Sunday afternoon when we was all lazing around the bunkhouse, a twister let down in the pasture right over there and come hell-bent right toward us, and we flattened out, but just before it got to the corral it lifted and went over us and the buildings and didn't harm anything. And while we were still on our knees, marveling, we noticed Parenthesis standing beside the corral, rolling a cigarette. There was no mistaking him on account of his uncommon bow legs.

We run to him and asked him where he'd been, and he said he took a little run over to the Rockies and then down to the Gulf of

Mexico and back. We asked him was he crazy and he said we couldn't imagine how good a cigarette tasted after all this time. He said he had everything else he needed. He even got so he could dip down and lift a cup of coffee off of a counter in a restaurant, out through the window, without spilling a drop, or damaging anything else. But he couldn't roll a cigarette in the middle of a cyclone.

We asked him if he got a bad knock on the head and he said he knew we thought he was crazy, but he broke that thing to ride. We asked him who did he think would believe that and he said he didn't blame us none for disbelieving, and all he come back for was his saddle. He was tired of riding the cyclone bareback.

We said he better come into the bunkhouse and lay down and get some rest. Somebody asked him what happened, did the horse buck him off, or did the cyclone pull him off of the horse. He said neither one. The cyclone sort of run up beside him and he got to wondering if he could ride it, so he jumped off the horse onto the cyclone.

He said it was real rough for an hour or two. The roughest ride he ever had. Then he kind of got the cyclone under control, and it learned fast. In a little while he could guide it by leaning this way or that way. The hardest thing was to keep it from putting its foot down where it would do damage. Even now he didn't like to ride it in a well settled country for fear it would set down on a house or something, so he kept out here in the cattle country mostly.

He said he hadn't figured any way to use the cyclone yet, except just to ride around on and see the country. But he had one idea that he had tried, and maybe could make a little cash. He could make a rock silo. He said he knew where there was a well about fifty feet deep, dug through solid rock, but it was dry and no good to anybody. So he set the funnel of the cyclone down on it and turned it wrong side out. It made a pretty silo, although it's way out in the pasture where there's no ensilage for miles around.

He said well he'd better breeze along, because he realized us boys would just tie him up and take him to the bughouse if he stayed around much longer. He went to the shed and got his saddle and walked out a little ways from the buildings and put his fingers in his mouth and whistled.

A black cloud come whirling toward us, and the funnel came down over the buildings, just missing them, and picked up Parenthesis. He took off his hat and waved and he was gone.

We didn't see anything of him for a while, then one day he dropped in on us again. He was all dressed up, and fat and prosperous, and he had a new silver-mounted saddle. He said he was really making a good thing out of it, herding rain clouds.

He would go down to the gulf coast where there's lots of clouds, and cut out a herd of them maybe fifteen, twenty miles wide. Then he'd push them to west Texas and New Mexico, wherever the ranchers needed rain. It took a lot of patience to herd rain clouds. It was like herding milk cows, if you run them they lost their rain. But after you got the knack of it, it was easy enough.

For rain he charged by the inch. A little spatter to settle the dust didn't cost much, but a half-inch rain come pretty high. A inch rain was more than twice as much as a half-inch rain, because it was so much more work, keeping the clouds bunched up and quiet for long enough to rain that much. Also you had to take time into consideration. A slow drizzle of say an inch was a lot more expensive than a sudden downpour of the same amount.

He said he had a few old clouds off to the northwest that had been just about all rained out and he would bring them over to cool us off a little, free. He asked about the strawberry roan, if his hair was growing back, and we said the roan was looking good. He said we could have the horse if we would promise to treat him right. Which we did.

Then he left, and soon the sky clouded over and it rained a little spatter, which cooled us off.

We was real sad when we found out how Parenthesis ended. It

seems he set his cyclone down on a saloon and lifted the whole stock, including a corkscrew. He wasn't exactly a drinking man, but he couldn't resist all that liquor whirling around him, so he opened a bottle. Seems when he had too much to drink he lost his judgment, like lots of other men, and he rode that cyclone over to the Rockies.

Well a cyclone don't like mountains any more than a horse likes rough ground. They stay mostly in flat land because it's easier going. But Parenthesis didn't figure how hard it was on his cyclone, and he rode it over the mountains and up and down from Canada to Mexico. And he broke its wind.

A wind-broke cyclone ain't any good. Besides, there was another thing. This cyclone was with whirlwind. I don't know whether or not he knew about its condition, but he should have. Anyway it gave birth to a litter of whirlwinds and died on him.

And there he was, five thousand feet up, with nothing to support him but some little whirlwinds not hardly big enough to blow a man's hat off. I guess he was dead drunk by this time and never knew what happened. I hope so. He hit awful hard.

The strawberry roan has got a nice glossy coat of hair now and his tail and mane is as long as any horse's. There's nothing wrong with him except he bucks when you first get on him.